FRIEDRICH NIETZSCHE

THE
DIONYSIAN
VISION
OF
THE
WORLD

TRANSLATED BY IRA J. ALLEN
INTRODUCTION BY FRIEDRICH ULFERS

UNIVOCAL

"Die dionysische Weltanschauung"
Friedrich Nietzsche,
1928 Leipzig, Richard Hadl

Translated by Ira J. Allen
as "The Dionysian Vision of the World"

First Edition
Minneapolis © 2013, Univocal Publishing
Published by Univocal
123 North 3rd Street, #202
Minneapolis, MN 55401
www.univocalpublishing.com

Designed & Printed by Jason Wagner
Distributed by the University of Minnesota Press

ISBN 9781937561024
Library of Congress Control Number: 2013930205

TABLE OF CONTENTS

Translator's Preface

Any translation owes its existence to some forebears; the stronger a translation, the more it owes. In this case, Nietzsche's striking early essay, "Die dionysische Weltanschauung," has found capable expression in English at the hands of Claudia Crawford, and has been rendered by Ronald Speirs as well. Also, Nietzsche used several sections from the essay verbatim in *Geburt der Tragödie*, and these are thus given in Walter Kaufmann's *The Birth of Tragedy*. The present translation has benefited from these predecessors as well as from conversations with Fred Ulfers, whose critical introduction is a valuable resource in its own right. This edition, *The Dionysian Vision of the World*, is nonetheless a fresh look at the text, committed above all to the task of translation as minimal interpretation of an original. The translated text, that is to say, is charged with presenting the same interpretive dilemmas, enigmas, and difficulties—or as close as possible—as are found in the original. Accordingly, in some instances where Crawford, Speirs, and Kaufmann have made strong interpretive decisions (most notably in rendering multivalent terms such as *Schein*, discussed here in note 3, but also via strategic capitalization and italicization), I have sought terms and phrases that might better present in English the ambiguities found in the original. The exception to this policy is the capitalization of "Will"; because Nietzsche shifts between speaking of the will in an everyday sense and in the technical sense particular to his philosophy, I have followed other translators in emphasizing the latter (a typographic innovation impossible in German, which capitalizes all nouns alike). It is my hope (expressed more fully in note 16) that some ambiguity remains all the same. Equally, I have worked to retain the birdsong resonances between various root-words chattering back and forth behind the text's melody, making Nietzsche's text itself an "incomparable harmony." With the caveat that any work of significance presents a lifetime's worth of such resonances, the reader will find some of the key linguistic and historical-philosophical linkages discussed in endnotes. Finally, it bears mention that I have followed Nietzsche's own typographic preference (preserved in Giorgio Colli and Mazzino Montinari's *Kritische Studienausgabe* edition of the text, from which this translation has benefited): marking emphasis by spacing, rather than italicization. Given Nietzsche's commitment to tonos, literally a stretching (see notes 8, 9 and 34), this spacing—which Univocal Publishing is uniquely well-suited to re-present—underscores the text's musical quality. *The Dionysian Vision of the World* must be at once both about music and itself musical.

INTRODUCTION
by Friedrich Ulfers

In *The Dionysian Vision of the World*, Nietzsche lays out an understanding of the becoming[1] of the world as an aesthetic process, an understanding that will run through all his later philosophy. In all the writings leading up to and including *The Birth of Tragedy*, there is always a reference to some aesthetic form (such as tragedy itself).[2] The only text among these to refer to an actual vision of the world is this one: *The Dionysian Vision of the World*. The vision Nietzsche offers here is not an aesthetics that relates to an innerworldly, i.e., human sensibility. As we will see, this is an aesthetics *of the world*.

---

1 "Becoming" [*Werden*] is the *Erlösung* or relief of what Nietzsche calls, in *The Birth of Tragedy*, the *Ur-Eine*, a "primordial unity" of opposites that is the source of all becoming. The world becomes *as* seeming, as *Schein*, relieving the painful overfullness of the *Ur-Eine*, a being that is divided in its very being. The *Ur-Eine* is not precisely being or non-being, but rather an *Unruhe* or inquietude that is always ready to manifest as a world of appearance. Becoming or *Werden* is this inquietude of being divided against itself relieving itself as appearance or *Schein*.
2 These include, crucially, two lectures and an essay from 1870, the same year Nietzsche completed *The Dionysian Vision of the World*: "Greek Musical Drama" and "Socrates and Tragedy," and "The Birth of Tragic Thought," respectively. Equally important for the development of Nietzsche's thought at this point are the essay "On Truth and Lies in an Extramoral Sense" and the unfinished volume *Philosophy in the Tragic Age of the Greeks*, both from 1873. *The Birth of Tragedy*, first published in 1872, was reissued in 1874 and 1878, and published in its final edition, a "New Edition with an Attempt at a Self-Critique," in 1886.

1

So, when Nietzsche talks about the world being an aesthetic phenomenon, he is not talking about the world being there for human perceiving. Rather, the world is aesthetic in its very becoming, in a fashion that cannot be restricted to or fully contained by human experiencing. It is this aesthetic immoderation that is grasped by the Dionysian vision of the world. One could almost call this an ontology of music[3]: where an "incomparable harmony" that is *not only* consonance, but also dissonance, serves as the source of the world's becoming. Nietzsche talks here about the simultaneity of coming into being and passing away, which, although they occur together, are not identical. This is a cosmological perspective, from which music appears as prior to phenomena, prior to appearance. Beyond conceptual language, there is a language of music that operates as an immediate or direct echo of a strictly ungraspable nature. Here, music is a matter of the primordial and asymmetrical entanglement of dissonance and consonance. The world comes to be as an aesthetic, musical process, an incomparable harmony comprised of both dissonant and consonant notes.

Nietzsche begins to lay out his aesthetic cosmology or ontology, which apprehends the world as an "aesthetic phenomenon" (*BT* 8.64), by stating that nature is an artist.[4] Nature is an artist insofar as two artistic energies,

---

3 Christoph Cox does just that in his contribution to *A Companion to Nietzsche* (Ed. Keith Ansell Pearson), "Nietzsche, Dionysus, and the Ontology of Music" (Oxford: Blackwell Publishing), 495-513.

4 In reading *The Dionysian Vision of the World*, I have had frequent recourse to Nietzsche's elaboration on certain key points in *The Birth of Tragedy*. The latter text incorporates verbatim large sections from this earlier essay, and thus offers illumination of many of those sections. This said, *The Dionysian Vision of the World* does stand on its own as a text and, indeed, may refigure certain of our understandings of *The Birth of Tragedy*. To accomplish that refiguring,

the Apollonian and the Dionysian, burst forth from nature herself "*without the mediation of the human artist*" (*BT* 2.38, cf. 4-5). These energies, named after the Greek gods Apollo and Dionysus, satisfy "nature's art impulses in the most immediate and direct way" (*BT* 2.38) and structure the world with two art forms: the imagistic Apollonian art of painting, sculpture, and the epic, and the non-imagistic Dionysian art of music. Nature, then, is first and foremost a certain need or desire for "worlding" or manifesting by way of aesthetics or art. What is at stake here is a compulsion to manifest that is rooted not in lack but in overfullness; this is an "immoderation" or *Übermaß* of nature herself. Nature "worlds" or becomes in two opposing styles, which merge in "the art of tragedy in the blossoming of the Hellenic 'Will'" (29).[5] The Will as such, which is a "primordial unity" (*BT, passim*) of being and not-being, relieves itself of the pain of overfullness by manifesting as a world of coming into being and passing away. The Apollonian urge to art hides this world of becoming, precisely through its own emphasis on appearance. In creating a world of beautiful seeming, the Apollonian distracts itself from precisely that which is the exemplary focus of the Dionysian: the temporariness of nature's worlding. The Hellenic "Will," a subset of the greater Will of nature, reaches its high point in the merger of the two styles.

---

however, is not my aim here. I quote the Kaufmann translation of *The Birth of Tragedy* with *BT*, by section and page. References to the present text are given by page number only.

5 The Hellenic "Will," which Nietzsche places in quotation marks, is but one cultural manifestation—albeit a tremendously significant one—of that primordial willing that is nature herself. This is the acculturation of nature's own art impulses.

3

The Beautiful Seeming
of the Apollonian Dreamworld

Nietzsche assigns the artwork of sculpture, painting, and the epic to the Apollonian and of music to the Dionysian, and he attributes the following states to Apollo and Dionysus, respectively: "*dreams*" and "*intoxication*" (29). What characterizes the Apollonian dreamworld is "seeming," *Schein* (29), which has a range of meanings, all the way from luminosity to veiling or covering up. Thus, there is the sense of beauty in its meaning of radiance, of a sheen or gloss. This Apollonian seeming or emphasis on beautiful appearance works as a sort of secondary appearing of a world that itself comes into being not as substance, but only ever as "mere" appearance. It is Dionysian intoxication that comes closest to grasping the insubstantive primary appearing that is all that world is.

Schein also alludes to propriety or good form, which allows us to immediately understand a "*figure*" or *Gestalt* (29); it is Schein that enables us to apprehend "figures" instantly and without mediating concepts or ideas. Then there is the epithet of Apollo as the "shining one," *der Scheinende* (30), "in his deepest roots the god of sun and light who reveals himself in radiance" (30). The clarity of light that is Apollo's domain makes him the god of "true cognition," of *wahre Erkenntnis*, including cognition of the unified self, since light gives clear-cut contours to what is to be cognized. This latter aspect makes him the god of the "*principium individuationis*" (31), that principle which insists that every entity must be self-enclosed and not subject to any admixture that would make it self-contradictory. Apollonian seeming is thus governed by the principles of non-contradiction and individuation, whereas Dionysian ecstasy is, as we will see, precisely the falling away of these principles.

Also, the art of the Apollonian dreamworld focuses on stasis, where Nietzsche sees the sculpture of Phidias as celebrating. He describes this sculpture as "completely immobile beauty" (33). More generally, the Apollonian valorizes the notion of substance: in the form of "persisting" (*Beharrendes*, *KSA* 8.458)[6] and "abiding" (*Bleibendes*, *KSA* 7.492). Apollo reigns over these as god of "the permanence of the world," the *Weltbestand* (*KSA* 7.240), god of "the radiant glorification of the eternity of the phenomenon" (*BT* 16.104). The appearance of appearance, namely, Apollonian seeming, makes for something that we could call a "substance ontology." It refers to at least a quasi-permanence and anchors this in a posited absolute permanence [*Sein* or Being]. A substance ontology wants to grasp the reality of being, but the world of becoming does not allow for such grasping.

Apollonian beautiful seeming extends, then, also to the Platonic notion of Being [*to ontōs on*], as espoused by Diotima in the *Symposium*. Diotima relates the "beautiful" to the concept of "form," whose beauty consists in the fact that it "always *is*" (211a).[7] Form's permanence refuses any past and any future; it always is present, and can be represented. "First, it always is and neither comes to be nor passes away, neither waxes nor wanes." Beauty as "form" is in no way relative or contingent: "it is not beautiful this

---

6 Scholars of Nietzsche are indebted to Giorgio Colli and Mazzino Montinari for their monumental collection of his work in the *Kritische Studienausgabe*, cited here as *KSA* with volume followed by page number.
7 I work here from Alexander Nehamas and Paul Woodruff's translation of the *Symposium* (Indianapolis: Hackett Publishing Company, 1989).

way and ugly that way, nor beautiful at one time and ugly at another, nor beautiful in relation to one thing and ugly to another, nor is it beautiful here but ugly there, as it would be were it beautiful for some people and ugly for others" (211a). That which is beautiful in itself is not, from this Platonic view, at all relative. Finally, "form," the "beautiful itself," is free of any mixture or pollution: "absolute, pure, unmixed, not polluted by human flesh or colors or any other great nonsense of mortality" (211e). By contrast, the Dionysian thrusts us directly into the coming to be and passing away of mortality, into what Plato calls "nonsense."[8]

Dionysus and the Intoxication of Suffering

Nietzsche ascribes "intoxication" to the Dionysian vision of the world, deriving this from the orgiastic nature cults of Thrace. Celebrating the "drive of springtime" and the Bacchanalia in honor of Dionysus, the god of "narcotic drink"—wine—Nietzsche interprets the term "intoxication" not as narcotic stupor but, on the contrary, as a kind of "rush," a *Rausch* that spells unboundedness. Intoxication is "ecstasy" taking place under the aegis of Dionysus as *ho lysios*—the "liberator"—who undoes boundaries. Dionysus sunders the Apollonian *principium individuationis* on which the unified conscious ego and oppositional couples are based. Speech—conceptual language (the *Begriff*)—is replaced by singing, and the

---

8 We fall into the realm of mortality, in the Judeo-Christian and other stories, because of guilt in another, Platonic realm of pure form. Nietzsche describes becoming in all innocence, but accepts that, while "it may not be logical ... it certainly is human, to view now, together with Anaximander, all coming-to-be as though it were an illegitimate emancipation from eternal being, a wrong for which destruction is the only penance" (*Philosophy in the Tragic Age of the Greeks*, 46; hereafter *Ph*). Nietzsche would relieve us of the guilt of becoming—passing away is a necessary part of the world because becoming, he says, is what the world *is*.

6

measured steps of walking are overtaken by dancing. Most important of all for Dionysus is the element of music—"Dionysian music," which consists of "the jarring force of tone and the absolutely incomparable world of harmony" (33). In Dionysian harmony, as Nietzsche interprets it, there is an *Unruhe*, an unquiet togetherness of dissonance and consonance.[9] For Nietzsche, harmony is contingent on what he refers to several times in *The Birth of Tragedy* as "dissonance." It is not a consonance of opposites, but rather a troubled unity, a unity that does not synthesize without remainder. Dionysian music is dissonantly harmonious, and in this serves as an immediate echo of a primordial and painfully overfull unity of pleasure and pain. It is not an aspect of the phenomenal world, but is "incomparable"—it cannot be compared to any phenomenon, but relates directly to the source of all becoming or appearing.

In the Dionysian intoxication of suffering, there is a general feeling of being transformed, of being out of stasis (from Greek *ek*[out of]-*stasis*) in the sense of being neither at one pole of a spectrum nor at the other. Nietzsche alludes to this "both-and" aspect of Dionysus and the effect he has on those in Dionysian ecstasy with phrases like "voluptuous nature celebrates its Saturnalia and its wakes simultaneously" (34) and "pain awakens pleasure, jubilation tears agonized tones from the breast" (34). These are themselves at once effects of Dionysian intoxication and the basic affects of a primordial unity, of

---

9 Nietzsche, of course, does not write "Unruhe," a key term of art for his philosophical rival, Hegel. Nonetheless, it is unquietness that is at stake here. On Hegelian *Unruhe*, restlessness or inquietude, see Jean-Luc Nancy, *Hegel: The Restlessness of the Negative*, Trans. Jason Smith and Steven Miller (Minneapolis: University of Minnesota Press, 2002).

nature in its becoming. These are hints that, in Dionysus and the Dionysian, opposites are no longer opposite, but form a "chiasmic unity"—a term derived from χ, the Greek letter "chi," and signifying irreducible entanglement. Chiasmic unity, by definition, violates the principle of non-contradiction, the principle upon which binary logic is based.[10] But this violation does not call for a "corrective" that would lead us back to binary logic. Rather, chiasmic unity is the domain of a different "logic," one prior to both contradiction and non-contradiction. Chiasmic logic suspends the system of binary opposition on which the principle of non-contradiction is based, but without reducing oppositions to some form of synthetic unity. In other words, chiasmic unity is a "one" that holds opposites together while simultaneously keeping them apart; it is the undecidability of their fusion and separation. In alluding to a chiasmic unity of opposites in the figure of Dionysus, Nietzsche follows Heraclitus, whom he acknowledges is closest to his own thinking.[11]

The Influence of Heraclitus

The tenets of Heraclitus that Nietzsche recognized as applicable to Dionysus and the Dionysian vision of the world are (as paraphrased by Nietzsche in *Philosophy in the Tragic Age of the Greeks*) the following:

1. Heraclitus' dictum that everything forever has its opposite along with it. "For this," according to Nietzsche, "Aristotle accused him of the highest crime before the

---

10   Barbara Johnson offers a useful consideration of chiasmic unity in *A World of Difference* (Baltimore: Johns Hopkins University Press, 1987), esp. 114-15. This also finds discussion, as "chaosmos," in Christoph Cox, *Nietzsche: Naturalism and Interpretation* (Berkeley and Los Angeles: University of California Press, 1999).
11   In *Ecce Homo*, 729-30.

highest tribunal of reason: to have sinned against the law of contradiction" (*Ph* 52). Nietzsche comments that this Heraclitean "truth" is not arrived at by "reason" and thus by the "law of contradiction," but by way of a "con-tuitive view" [*Zusammenschauen*] (*Ph* 61) that sees opposites connected without fusing them, i.e., as an "entanglement" [*Ineinander*] (*KSA* 7.213).

2. The denial of the "duality of totally diverse worlds," i.e., the refusal to distinguish "a physical world from a metaphysical one" (*Ph* 51).

3. The denial of a static "Being" (*Ph* 51). This is a reference back to the Platonic notion of the permanence of that which simply is. Via Heraclitus, Nietzsche is rejecting a Platonic opposition between *Sein* (Being) and *Schein* (appearing), between *Seienden* (existents) and *Erscheinungen* (phenomena), an opposition in which Being simply *is*, outside of all time and appearance.

4. The affirmation of "becoming" (*Ph* 51) i.e., the everlasting and incessant coming-to-be and passing away, without any resolutive stasis of being (*Ph* 54).

5. "The strife of opposites [that] gives birth to all that comes to be" (*Ph* 55). This tension, a *polemos* or kind of war, is leading not only toward some deathblow but is also creative. This strife is a tension of overfullness, much like pregnancy—for Heraclitus, strife is not negative, but affirmatively generative.

6. The notion of "contradictions run[ning] into harmony" (*Ph* 61). Here, we have in Heraclitus what Nietzsche calls "incomparable harmony." Life in its

construction and destruction is eternal, but not in a Judeo-Christian sense of life after death—rather, contradictions run into harmony in the eternal liveliness of construction-destruction cycles.

7. Destruction as an integral part of the "ever self-renewing impulse" in a "game" that life plays with itself in which "coming-to-be and passing away" are modes of "structuring and destroying, without any moral additive, forever in equal innocence" (*Ph* 62). Via innocent destruction, life renews itself. The game that Nietzsche refers to is that which Zeus plays as a child: he constructs a sand-castle and, when sated, destroys it in order to start over again.[12]

8. The "play of antinomies" with propositions such as "we are and at the same time are not the same" or "being and non-being is at the same time the same and not the same" (*Ph* 77). These contradictions or paradoxes characterize the philosophy of Heraclitus, and are always associated with what he calls "harmony" (*harmoniē*).[13]

Before going on to show how Dionysus turns out to be the very "figure" of chiasmic unity—along the lines suggested

12 In one of "Five Introductions to Five Unwritten Books," written in 1872 for Cosima Wagner (specifically, in "On the Pathos of Truth"), Nietzsche describes Heraclitus as attending, like no other mortal before him, to "the play of the great world-child [*Weltenkind*] Zeus and thus to the eternal sport of world-disintegration [*Weltzertrümmerung*] and world-emergence [*Weltentstehung*]" (*KSA* 1.758).
13 See Charles Kahn, *The Art and Thought of Heraclitus. An Edition of the Fragments with Translation and Commentary* (Cambridge: Cambridge University Press, 1979), for a view of harmony as a "specifically Heraclitean notion of the structure or fitting together of the cosmic order as a unity produced from conflict" (197).

by this list of Heraclitean tenets—I first turn to Nietzsche's account of the Dionysian eruption upon the scene of Apollonian culture. It is crucial to understand how this encounter led to the Dionysian "wisdom of suffering" (37). In this wisdom, which is ecstatic intoxication, chiasmic nature expresses itself; it does so in the artwork of tragedy and of music.

The Seriousness of Greek Religion

Nietzsche traces the roots of Dionysus to a cult in his honor in Thrace, which resettled in the Apollonian culture of the Homeric-Greek world. The Greeks tamed the "rawest unleashing of the lowest drives" (32) that occurred, as already mentioned, during orgiastic celebration of the rites of spring and Bacchanalian services. This Dionysian nature-cult was marked by "sexual licentiousness" and "unbounded hetaerism" (35). Thus, it amounted to an "idealization of the orgy" (32) when, under the aegis of Apollo, the Hellenes integrated Dionysus and his cult of "intoxication" into their ritual life, to the extent of dividing certain annual functions between Apollo and Dionysus. Nietzsche leaves no doubt that this act of assimilating the Dionysian to the Apollonian is not to be understood as the sort of *laissez-faire* "playing around" [*Spielerei*] of which the "religion of the Greeks"—Apollo and the Olympian gods—had often been accused (36).

Nietzsche vigorously contests the reductive interpretation of the Apollonian dreamworld that had been common among scholars. He does readily admit that Greek "religion" is not "serious" in a moral sense, the sense of following certain edicts that prohibit and allow

11

only certain actions, or declare behavior to be either good or evil. Rather, Greek religion is serious about "an often unrecognized ... wisdom" (36), namely, that suffering and pain necessarily accompany individual existence and, more generally, the world of "phenomena" (*BT* 17.104) or "appearances" (*BT* 16.104). This suffering stems from the fact that phenomena are always passing away. The beauty and lightheartedness of Apollonian religion are intimately related to, even based upon, the pain and suffering of a fleeting world of appearances. Nietzsche describes this in terms of an insight into the "perpetual destruction" (*BT* 8.62) and the "ceaseless flux of appearances" (*BT* 16.104), and into the fact "that all that comes into being must be ready for a sorrowful end" (*BT* 17.104). What Nietzsche is claiming is that the Homeric-Greek world understood this suffering; the beautiful Apollonian pantheon has to do with insight into the inherent pain of a sorrowful end. As evidence, he cites a lament for "short-lived Achilles" in the *Iliad* (38)—an indication of the poet's awareness of human deathboundness, a horror that must be veiled so that one might go on living.

"The *pain* of Homeric man [that] was bound to departure from ... existence ... is to be hidden by the radiant form" of Apollo (37-38). That is, Apollo himself serves as a beautiful cover for the painfulness of a world of transient appearances. "For how else could such a people, so infinitely sensitive, so brilliant in their capacity for suffering, have borne existence if this itself had not been revealed to them" in the Apollonian seeming of beauty (34). A primordial fullness relieves itself by coming into being as a world of appearing and passing away, a world of suffering. The painfulness of this fact must be represented even as it is covered over. The Apollonian is not only a style devoted to beauty and serenity; that serenity itself is a deliberate cover for insight into the inherent suffering of short-lived existence. "To see ... existence as it actually is in a transfiguring mirror and to protect itself" (37) with this mirror from the pain and suffering of deathbound existence—this was the ingenious strategy of the Homeric Greeks, of the epic artwork and the unblemished sculpture.

For Nietzsche, the Homeric-Greek world, for which the Apollonian "sphere of beauty" is a way of dealing with its "background" (37)—the horror of the death and destruction of all that comes to be—makes of beauty a "weapon" with which to battle "that talent correlative to the [Apollonian], the talent for *suffering*" (39). In other words, Apollonian beauty is a weapon that corresponds in its effectivity to a Greek capacity for pain. The world of coming to be and of passing away, the "mere" appearance that is all that any world is, produces suffering and thus has to be guarded against. The Homeric Greeks, says Nietzsche, are unusually attuned to this fact and the beauty of Apollonian dreaming, the "appearance of appearances" that we cannot help but regard as reality (*KSA* 1. 39), is the weapon with which they guarded themselves. This battle takes place against their own sense of the phenomenal world [*Erscheinungswelt*], away from which the Dionysian vision draws the veil. As we have seen, in the Heraclitean configuration adopted by Nietzsche, the Dionysian vision of the world is more direct. This is an intoxicated but clear-eyed vision of radical becoming, of "everlasting and incessant coming-to-be and passing away" (*Ph* 54), of the chiasmic unity or simultaneity of being and non-being. The suffering related to this vision of world as eternal becoming, which implies that everything which comes to be is soon destroyed—alluded to as the "background"—comes out into the open in the battle of the Apollonian against the Dionysian, of beautiful seeming against the "truth" of suffering. It is Silenus, the "forest god" (36), who emblematizes this dangerous coming into the open, which could lead to an absolute disgust for the world.

The Wisdom of Silenus

Silenus, a companion of Dionysus, is thus part of the Dionysian force that, as "intoxication" or "ecstasy," had threatened to overrun Homeric Apollonian culture and all its measures and boundaries. However, as we have already noted, this force was tamed by Apollonian culture, integrated, allowed to have celebrations in honor of Dionysus side by side with those for Apollo and to enter the sphere of art by way of Dionysian music. This said, Silenus still poses a problem. He speaks out about the "truth" of the suffering that lies beneath Apollo's beautiful seeming, saying that living is dying and dying living, concluding with the advice: "Best is not to be, second-best to die quickly" (37). He points out what it would mean for us if we did not develop some wisdom of suffering; he is, then, the figure who embodies the horror of unending coming to be while passing away. The question is how the Dionysian vision manages to overcome the disgust at living that might be prompted by Dionysus' companion.

Nietzsche interprets Silenus' pessimistic message as a "truthful" insight, as a point of departure from which the Dionysian makes inroads into Apollonian culture. But Silenus is only a moment in the process of accepting the appearing of a world that is nothing more than appearance. What Nietzsche has in mind is a penetration of the Apollonian by the Dionysian that embodies, as an extension of Silenus' "truth," the intoxicated-ecstatic disposition that envisions everything, including "truth" itself, as chiasmic unity. The wisdom of suffering at the heart of the Dionysian vision develops a different kind of truth, wherein what Silenus describes directly and without adornment as suffering is ecstatically entangled with its opposite, becoming painful pleasure.[14] The Dionysian view of suffering must always be a double view, a chiasmic view.

In confronting this Dionysian truth, Apollonian beautiful seeming falls short. With its attempt to eternalize the individual and the world of appearances, and with all that "thus far counted as limits, as measuring determination" founding the "truth" of the principle of non-contradiction, the beauty of Apollo "proved itself here but artificial seeming [*künstlischer Schein*]" (42). Here, then, what is artificial and what is artistic cannot be neatly separated. That is to say, the "artistic seeming" [*künstlischer Schein*] of Apollo, celebrated in the artwork of sculpture, painting, and the epic (38) and based on simplicity or moderation— "*medēn āgan*" (42)[15]—turns out to be an artifice for veiling the complex, immoderate "truth" of Dionysus. This "truth" always already exceeds the moderation of the Apollonian "truth" by being a contradiction that is not a logical, but rather a chiasmic, ontological one. It is in the ecstatic "self-forgottenness" [*Selbstvergessenheit*] (43) of the Dionysian state, as an ontological structure, that

---

14 Nietzsche's view thus finds an echo in Derridean "undecidability," which is, for example, an "excess"—a "painful pleasure ... which partakes of both good and ill, of the agreeable and the disagreeable." *Dissemination*, Trans. Barbara Johnson (London: Continuum, 2004), 102. Nietzsche himself, of course, further develops his view of truth's contingency in "On Truth and Lies in an Extramoral Sense."

15 This Delphic wisdom translates literally as "nothing immoderately."

"'immoderation' laid itself bare as the truth!" (42). Here, "contradiction, the bliss born of pain, spoke out from the very heart of nature" (*BT* 4.46-47). The "heart of nature" Nietzsche speaks of here is also called the "Will" (43), the "world of the Will" (62), the "primordial unity" (BT *passim*), the "essence of nature" (55), the "essence of the thing" (55), the "essential being [*Wesen*] of appearances" (38). Primordiality is not Being, but that *Unruhe* or immoderation or overfullness that could be called a creative tension. This is not just creative tension in an individual human being or even specific to the human species; rather, at the heart of nature is some creative desiring, a Will [*Wille*] or a wanting [*Wollen*] to manifest.[16]

The Divided Heart of Nature

In contrasting the "heart of nature"—the "Will" or "primordial unity"—with "appearance," Nietzsche is not participating in the traditional Western opposition of Being and appearance [*Sein* and *Schein*], all references to "essence" notwithstanding. In the progression from the pessimistic wisdom of Silenus regarding suffering and pain to a fuller Dionysian wisdom, it is necessary to realize that the latter is gained by an *interpretation* of the suffering of incessant coming to be and passing away as "*intoxication*" (39). Dionysus "interpreted the enigma and the horror of the world in tragedy and expressed in tragic music the innermost thoughts of nature, the weaving of the

---

16 What Nietzsche calls "Will" here later becomes a "Will to power," a *Wille zur Macht*. This should not be interpreted in strictly human terms—far from it—but rather as a desire-to-manifest, a potentiality-pathos that possibilizes the world of becoming. In *The Human Condition*, Hannah Arendt notes something of the sort, observing that "The word ["power"] itself, its Greek equivalent *dynamis*, like the Latin *potentia* with its various modern derivatives or the German *Macht* (which derives from *mögen* and *möglich*, not from *machen*), indicates its 'potential' character" (Chicago: University of Chicago Press, 1958), 200.

'Will' in and beyond all appearances" [*Erscheinungen*] (33). The Will is not simply "beyond" but also "in" appearances. As the Will actualizes itself, it is simultaneously beyond but also just as much *in* and *of* appearances, coming to be and passing away.

Dionysian wisdom interprets the suffering inherent in the world as an integral aspect of the "heart of nature," of the "Will" as the "ground" of all phenomena, in terms of intoxication or ecstasy. This can only mean the following: The Will's suffering is at the very core of that immoderation that does not abide by the principles of non-contradiction and *principium individuationis*. Rather, the chiasmic unity of opposites—the Heraclitean "union of opposites"— discussed earlier in conjunction with the affinity of the Dionysian and Heraclitean visions of the world, is apprehensible in and through an ecstatic uptake of suffering. In other words, the intoxication of suffering that echoes the emotion of the "Will" or "primordial unity" entails the entanglement of pain *and* pleasure. Here, the Dionysian vision of the world overcomes Silenus' disgust at the pain of the world. The "contradiction," following the Heraclitean dictum that "everything forever has its opposite along with it" (*Ph* 52), means that suffering, too, has its opposite with it. Thus it is that Nietzsche gives us a primally ecstatic "One" in which "bliss [is] born of pain" and vice versa (*BT* 4.46-47).

Nietzsche goes on to say that the Dionysian vision of the Will's pain-bliss connection is related to that Will's being "eternally suffering and contradictory" (*KSA* 1.38). This suffering Will, the inessential essence of nature, "needs the rapturous vision, pleasurable seeming, for its continuous relief" (*KSA* 1.38). We are "wholly captured by and comprised of this seeming," which we are compelled to apprehend as "empirical reality," in other words, as "that which is truly not, an ongoing becoming in time, space, and causality" (*KSA* 1.38-39). There is, properly speaking, no "empirical reality," but only becoming. The "Will" that drives this becoming, then, must be understood as a *pathos*,[17] in the sense of an "overfullness" of pleasure and pain, which is, as such, simultaneously an "ardent longing for seeming, to be relieved through appearances" (*KSA* 1.38). It is as pathos rather than substance that the Will finds relief from its overfullness of pleasure and pain by manifesting itself in "seeming," as a world that "is truly not," i.e., as "perpetual becoming" (*KSA* 1.39). Once again, Nietzsche is following Heraclitean tenets: the "Dionysian Will" (49), as "contradiction," is a "strife" out of which the world of phenomena [*Erscheinungswelt*] as perpetual becoming is born. To put it differently, the Dionysian Will, as "strife," is a suffering from the overfullness of self-contradiction that finds relief in the "pleasure" of seeming or appearances [*Schein*]. What is important to note here is that, for Nietzsche, the "appearances" generated by the Dionysian Will's primordial desire to find relief through seeming [*Schein*] precede, as it were, the beautiful seeming of Apollo's dreamworld. As Nietzsche puts it, "If we glance away from our own 'reality' for even an instant, conceiving of our empirical existence, as also of the world's in general, as a continuously generated presentation of the primordial unity [*Ur-Eine*], we shall then have to take the dream to be the *seeming* of *seeming*, a still higher satisfaction of the primordial desire for appearances" (*KSA* 1.39).

---

17 Toward the end of his conscious career, in the notebooks of 1888 and 1889, Nietzsche makes clear that "the Will to power is not a being, not a becoming, but rather a pathos—and, as such, is the most elementary of facts, out of which emerges all becoming, all effecting" (*KSA* 13.260).

As a pathos, the "Will" Nietzsche evokes here is neither more nor less than the suffering of overfullness and the relief of manifesting. The "Dionysian Will" is, then, "compared to the Apollonian, the eternal and artistic power that first calls the whole world of phenomena [the world of coming-to-be and passing-away] into existence—and it is only in the midst of this world that a new transfiguring illusion becomes necessary, in order to keep the animated world of individuation alive" (*BT* 25.143, cf. 13). In the Apollonian, it is almost as though the primordial unity were taking pity on human frailty. Via the Apollonian, the Will has another task—to keep us in the business of living on by helping hold the disgust of Silenus at bay even as we move through it. What Nietzsche is leading up to here is that Dionysian wisdom, aside from laying bare the immoderation of nature's Will, also generates its own "seeming." In other words, the Dionysian Will and the Apollonian are both involved in the production of "seeming." As Nietzsche puts it, "All that is actual gives way to seeming [*Schein*] and behind it is announced the *unitary nature of the Will*" (49). After identifying both the Dionysian and the Apollonian with "seeming," Nietzsche proclaims that "these two manifestations of the Will had an extraordinary aim: to create a *higher possibility of existence*, and, also, to arrive in that at a *still higher glorification* (through art)" (49). What is at stake in such glorification is the development of what Nietzsche calls a "metaphysical comfort" that will not gloss over the suffering of coming to be and passing away (*BT* 7.59).

Tragedy's Higher Glorification

The higher glorification Nietzsche describes is "no longer the art of seeming, but rather tragic art" (53) and "Dionysian music" (36). Tragedy, for Nietzsche, means an acceptance and celebration of the eternal life of the

Will, in its creation and destruction. We become capable of such acceptance and celebration precisely through the destruction of the tragic hero. The purpose of this destruction is not necessarily to evoke, à la Aristotle, fear and pity, but is rather to glorify that which creates. Despite, or even because of, the tragic hero's demise, we come to venerate life, which keeps coursing on in and through destruction. Life eternally regenerates itself because of destruction. This helps explain how tragedy or the conception of the tragic, and also Dionysian music, function as routes to a "higher possibility of existence" and a "higher glorification" than the instruments of the Apollonian dreamworld are capable of producing.

What is essential here is Nietzsche's association of the tragic and music with the Dionysian, and more precisely with Dionysian wisdom in its merger with the Apollonian art impulse. We recall here the insight of that wisdom gained through the "intoxication of suffering," that is, that the chiasmic suffering of nature constitutes the Will: "the primordial contradiction and primordial pain, along with the primordial pleasure of seeming" (*KSA* 1.44). As Nietzsche puts it, "The Dionysian, with its primordial joy experienced even in pain, is the common source of music and tragic myth" (*BT* 24.141). What, then, is the "higher glorification" that is supposed to occur in tragedy and music? With regard to the tragic myth, which relates the suffering of the tragic hero, Nietzsche proposes the following: there is an ecstatic Dionysian insight into the Will as a chiasmic unity of suffering and pleasure. The suffering of the Will is simultaneous with the Will's joy or relief in manifesting itself as "appearance," i.e., as a phenomenal world that is simultaneously a coming-to-be and a passing-away, a world always being annihilated.

The "metaphysical comfort" offered by tragedy is an attunement to the "eternal life of that core of existence, the ever-ongoing going under [*Untergang*] of phenomena" (*KSA* 1.59). What Nietzsche claims for "higher glorification" is that it is first through the tragic, with its conception of the "intoxication of suffering" and "Dionysian wisdom," that we can understand the joy involved in the annihilation of the individual:

> For it is only in particular examples of such annihilation that we see clearly the eternal phenomenon of Dionysian art, which gives expression to the Will ... behind the *principium individuationis*, the eternal life beyond all phenomena, and despite all annihilation. The ... joy in the tragic is the translation of the instinctive, unconscious Dionysian wisdom into the language of images: the [tragic] hero ... is negated for our pleasure, because he is only phenomenon, and because the eternal life of the Will is not affected by his annihilation. (*BT* 16.104)

The tragic hero is not to be pitied; he is annihilated for our pleasure. We are to be thankful that he embodies the eternal phenomenalization of the Will's suffering and pleasure. In other words, Nietzsche upends the Aristotelian definition of tragedy, which relies on fear, pity and catharsis.[18]

---

18 For Aristotle, tragedy is famously "an imitation of an action that is serious, complete, and of a certain magnitude" that through "pity and fear" effects "the proper purgation [catharsis] of these emotions," so long as the tragic hero be sufficiently noble and the appropriate moral compass be restored by play's end. *Poetics*, Trans. S.H. Butcher (New York: Hill and Wang, 1961), 61. By contrast, the demise of the tragic hero is for Nietzsche an *aesthetic* phenomenon, not a moral one. Indeed, Nietzsche sneers at the Aristotelian notion that, through tragedy, "we are supposed to feel elevated and inspired by the triumph of good and noble principles" (*BT* 22.132). Quite the contrary, he claims. To feel this way is "to have had no experience of tragedy as a supreme *art*" (*BT* 22.132).

To the extent that catharsis does occur here, it involves the joy that *only* phenomena are destroyed. At its core, life—as the coming to be and passing away of phenomena, as neither more nor less than the ambivalently productive pathos of nature or Will—goes on forever.

On Music as Immediate Symbolization of the Will

The role of music, or, more specifically, of "Dionysian music," in terms of "higher glorification" derives, like the tragic, from "Dionysian wisdom," i.e., from insight into the chiasmic unity of the Will. However, the difference between tragic art and Dionysian music is important. Whereas tragic myth conveys the Dionysian wisdom regarding the eternal life of the Will despite and through all annihilation, it does so in the language of images. Dionysian music, however, symbolizes the Will outside of and prior to the world of appearances, that is, outside the realm of "image-making or visual art" (57), in a domain where the Will "makes itself immediately understandable" (55). In other words, music does not refer to "a phenomenon of the Will [*Willenserscheinung*]" (59), to one or another moment of seeming, but to the "truly existent" world of the Will as this itself generates phenomena, "appearances" (57).

Now, there is something strange about Nietzsche's wording here. If the heart of nature is a *Wollen*, a willing or wanting, it cannot be "truly existent" in the sense of substance. We can only imagine that Nietzsche means that the *Ur-Eine*, that "primordial unity" driving all appearing, all becoming, is itself not an appearing or a becoming. The truly existent, then, is *neither* some form of static Being [*Sein*] *nor* the specific ephemera of Appearing [*Schein*]. It is truly existent insofar as it never belongs to the appearances that it generates; and yet "existence" still does not denote substance or grounding being. The primordial unity is not part of the *Erscheinungswelt*, and yet the phrase "truly existent" should not seduce us into believing that Nietzsche addresses a fullness behind all appearances. Rather, what is at stake here is a sort of subtraction from appearances, something that is no *thing* at all, but a *pathos*, a feeling.[19] It is in this sense that Dionysian music can be the "*symbolism ... of the world*" (58); it is the immediate echo of the world in its symbolizing activity of worlding. Music is immediate, is itself the productive activity of the feeling Will, taken as symbol, rather than being a set of symbols produced by the Will in its manifestation as appearance. This is the Dionysian sounding of the world.

So, what is it in Dionysian music that makes it an "immediate" symbol of the Will, of the chiasmus of pleasure and pain? Nietzsche lists "harmony" (54) and "musical dissonance" (*BT* 24.141) as the key characteristics of Dionysian music. With the idea of "harmony," he undoubtedly has in mind the harmony of contrary motion, i.e., the simultaneous movement of tones in opposite directions, where one line moves up and the other down at the same time. A likely source for this sense of harmony as proceeding from and via contradiction is Heraclitus' understanding of it as the unlike being joined together. For Heraclitus, harmony is a matter of "graspings: wholes and not wholes, convergent divergent, consonant dissonant, from all things one and from one thing all" (CXXIV, in *Art and Thought of Heraclitus*, 85). In these impossible graspings, "the counter-thrust brings together, and from tones at variance

---

19 There is no escaping the fact that this is a reference to something psychical. For a fuller exposition of Nietzsche's panpsychism, see Friedrich Ulfers and Mark Cohen, "Nietzsche's Panpsychism as the Equation of Mind and Matter" (forthcoming).

comes perfect attunement, and all things come to pass through conflict" (LXXV, in *Art and Thought*, 63). Harmony has for Nietzsche, from this Heraclitean perspective, the same relation to Dionysian wisdom as musical dissonance (*BT* 24.141).[20] Namely, the feeling, scarcely imagistic insight of Dionysus apprehends the Will as a joining-together of unlikes, the chiasm of primordial joy and pain, the contradiction or strife that is the source of all that comes to be and passes away. It is in this, as Nietzsche puts it, that music serves as "the Dionysian mirror of the world" (*BT* 19.119) and becomes "endow[ed] ... with a Dionysian-cosmic mission" (*BT* 19.119). Finally, what is at stake for Nietzsche in this essay is that the art of Dionysian music is actively symbolizing the order of the world, which is itself an aesthetic phenomenon. Via his music, the Dionysian musician becomes one with that divided *Ur-Eine*, the primordial unity of the Will.

---

20 In *Music: An Appreciation, 6ᵗʰ Edition* (Columbus, OH: McGraw-Hill), Roger Kamien characterizes dissonance as "an unstable tone combination ... its tension demands an onward motion to a stable chord. Thus dissonant chords are 'active'; traditionally they have been considered harsh and have expressed pain, grief, and conflict" (41). Nietzsche's genius is to recognize in that pain, grief, and conflict a "primordial joy" (*BT* 24.141).

THE DIONYSIAN VISION OF THE WORLD

1.

The Greeks, who in their gods at once declare and conceal
the secret doctrine of their vision of the world,[1] established
two deities as the twinned source of all their art: Apollo
and Dionysus. In the domain of art, these names represent
opposing styles; nearly always entangled and entering
into struggle with one another, they appear merged but
once, in the blossoming of the Hellenic "Will" in the
artwork of Attic tragedy. All this is to say, the human
achieves the blissful feeling of existence[2] in two states: in
d r e a m s and in i n t o x i c a t i o n . The beautiful
seeming [*Schein*][3] of the dream world, in which every
person is the consummate artist, is the father of all the
imagistic arts and, as we shall see, also a good half of poetry.
We enjoy an immediate understanding of the f i g u r e
[*Gestalt*]; all forms speak to us; there is nothing indifferent
and unnecessary. Even in our utmost experiencing of this
dream-actuality, however, we have still the sensation of its
s e e m i n g , shimmering through. As soon as this
sensation is lost, pathological effects set in; the dream
no longer refreshes and the healing power of nature halts
its operation. Within these boundaries, however, it is not
merely those images that are agreeable and pleasant that
we—with that total comprehending—seek out within

ourselves. The severe, the sorrowful, the bleak, the obscure: all are viewed with the same pleasure. It is only that the veil of seeming must remain in fluttering motion, not fully concealing the basic forms of the actual. Whereas the dream is thus the individual human's play with what is actual, the art of the image-maker (in the broader sense) is p l a y   w i t h   t h e   d r e a m . The statue as a block of marble is something very actual, but the actuality of the statue a s   d r e a m - f i g u r e is the living person of the god. So long as the statue floats before the artist's eyes as a fantasy image, he plays still with the actual; when he translates this image into marble, he plays with the dream.

In what sense, then, was A p o l l o able to be made the god of a r t ? Only in his being the god of the dream-presentation.[4] He is the "shining one" [*der Scheinende*] through and through, in his deepest roots the god of sun and light who reveals himself in radiance. "Beauty" [*Schönheit*] is his element, eternal youth his companion. But the beautiful seeming [*schöner Schein*] of the dream-world is his domain, too; higher truth, the perfection of these conditions in contrast to day-to-day actuality's tattered intelligibility, elevates him to a prophesying[5] god, but just as surely to an artificing god. The god of beautiful seeming must be at the same time the god of true cognition [*der wahren Erkenntnis*]. But that delicate limit over which the dream-image may not step if it is not to function pathologically—where seeming does not merely cheat but defrauds—must not be missing from Apollo's essential being: that modest delimitation, that freedom from the wilder impulses, that wisdom and tranquility of the image-making god. His eye must be "sunnily" tranquil[6]; even when it glares and looks baleful, the benediction of beautiful seeming lies upon it.

Conversely, Dionysian art is centered on the play with intoxication, with the state of ecstasy. There are two powers above all else that elevate the naive men of nature to the self-forgetting of intoxication: the drive of springtime and narcotic drink. Their workings are symbolized in the figure of Dionysus. In both states, the *principium individuationis* is sundered and the subjective disappears entirely before the erupting force of the generally human, indeed, the common-to-all, the natural.[7] The festivals of Dionysus not only forge a union between man and man, but reconcile man and nature. The earth offers up its gifts freely, the wildest beasts approach peaceably; the flower-garlanded wagon of Dionysus is drawn by panthers and tigers. All the enclosing boundaries laid fast between persons by necessity and contingency disappear: the slave is a free man, the noble and the lowly-born unite in the same Bacchic choruses. In ever-greater throngs, the gospel of "the harmony of worlds"[8] rolls from place to place. Singing and dancing, the human manifests himself as member of a high, more ideal commonality; he has unlearnt walking and speech. But more: he feels himself enchanted and he has actually become something other. As the animals speak and the earth gives forth milk and honey, so there sounds out from him something supernatural. He feels himself a god; what else lives only in his power of imagination, he senses now within himself. What are images and statues to him now? The human is no longer artist, but has become artwork; he is as ecstatically and exaltedly transformed as before he saw the gods transformed in dreams. The artistic force of nature, no longer that of a human, now reveals itself—a nobler clay,[9] a more precious marble here is kneaded and hewn: the human. This human, formed by the artist Dionysus, stands in relation to nature as the statue does to the Apollonian artist.

Now, if intoxication is nature's play with the human, then the Dionysian artist's creating is play with intoxication. If one has not experienced it oneself, this state can only be grasped by analogy: it is similar to dreaming and at once feeling the dream to be a dream. Just so, the servant of Dionysus must himself be intoxicated and at the same time lying in wait behind himself, observing. It is not in alternation between clarity and intoxication, but in their entanglement, that Dionysian artistry shows itself.

This entanglement marks the high point of Hellenism. Originally, Apollo alone is the Hellenic god of art; it was his power that tempered Dionysus' storming out of Asia, so as to allow the most beautiful fraternal union to emerge. Here, one grasps most easily the incredible idealism of the Hellenic mode of being: out of a nature cult—which among the Orientals signified the rawest unleashing of the lowest drives, bursting for a certain time all social bonds—there grew for the Greeks a festival of world-redemption, a day of transfiguration. All the sublime drives of their mode of being reveal themselves in this idealization of the orgy.

Hellenism was never in greater danger, however, than it was when the new god stormily drew near. Never, moreover, did the wisdom of the Delphine Apollo show itself in a finer [schöner] light. Reluctantly at first, he wrapped his prodigious opponent in the most precious gossamer, that this other might scarce mark that he had marched halfway into captivity. Inasmuch as the Delphic priesthood grasped the new cult's profound effect on processes of social regeneration and promoted it according to their own political-religious intent, inasmuch as the Apollonian artist learned with deliberate moderation from the revolutionary art of the Bacchanalian service, inasmuch as dominion over the year in the Delphine order was ultimately divided between Apollo and Dionysus, both gods emerged as victors from their struggle, so to speak: a reconciliation upon the field of battle. If one would see quite clearly how violently the Apollonian element suppressed the irrational, supernatural aspect of Dionysus, however, one needs only to recall that, in the older musical era, the *gēnos dithyrambikōn* was also the *hesuchastikōn*. The more powerful the Apollonian artistic spirit now grew, the more freely did Dionysus, the brother-god, develop; in the time of Phidias, just as the former arrived at a completely immobile view of beauty [*Schönheit*], as it were, the latter interpreted the enigma and the horror of the world in tragedy and expressed in tragic music the innermost thoughts of nature, the weaving of the "Will" in and beyond all appearances [*Erscheinungen*].

If music is also Apollonian art, it is, strictly speaking, only rhythm whose power of i m a g e - m a k i n g was developed for representation of Apollonian states; the music of Apollo is architecture in tones,[10] and furthermore only in the allusive tones proper to the *cithara*. The very element that constitutes the character of Dionysian music—indeed, of music as such—is gingerly held at a distance: the jarring force of tone and the absolutely incomparable world of harmony. The Greeks had for these the finest sensibility, as we must conclude from the rigorous character of the m o d e s [*Tonarten*], even as the need for a fully e l a b o r a t e d , actually sounded harmony was much weaker among them than in the newer world. In the harmonic progression and already in its abbreviation, in so-called melody, the "Will" reveals itself quite immediately, without first having entered into some appearance [*Erscheinung*]. Each *individuum* can serve as a likeness, much as a particular case does for a general rule; conversely, the Dionysian artist would lay immediately bare the essential being [*Wesen*] of appearances [*Erscheinungen*]—indeed, he holds sway over the chaos of the not-yet-formed Will and, from it,[11] can in each creative moment make a new world, b u t a l s o t h e o l d , known as appearance [*Erscheinung*]. It is in the latter sense that he is a tragic musician.

In Dionysian intoxication, in the tumultuous dash through all the scales of the soul—in narcotic excitations or in the unleashing of the drives of spring—nature expresses itself in its greatest power: it clasps individual beings together once more and lets them feel themselves as one—such that the *principium individuationis* appears [*erscheint*] as something like a persistent weakness of the Will. The more dissolute the Will, the more all crumbles into individual pieces; the more self-willed the development of the *individuum*, the weaker the organism that it serves. In this state, something like a sentimental motion of the Will at once erupts, a "creature sigh" for what is lost—from out of the greatest pleasure[12] sounds [*tönt*] the cry of deepest dismay, the yearning wail of an irreparable loss. Voluptuous nature celebrates its Saturnalia and its wakes simultaneously. The affects of its priests are intermingled in the most wondrous fashion: pain awakens pleasure, jubilation tears agonized tones [*Töne*] from the breast. The god *ho lysios* has delivered everything from himself, transformed everything. The song and countenance of the masses aroused in this manner, through whom nature gained voice and movement, was for the Homeric-Greek world something entirely new and unheard-of; it was for this world something Oriental, something it had first to conquer by its own prodigious rhythmic and image-making power, just as it did the

34

Egyptian temple style, It was the Apollonian people who cast the overwhelming force of instinct into the fetters of beauty [*Schönheit*]; they brought the most dangerous elements of nature, its wildest beasts, under beauty's yoke. We marvel most at the idealistic power of Hellenism when we compare its spiritualization of the Dionysian celebration with what emerged from that same source among other peoples. Similar festivals are age-old and can be pointed to all over the world, most famously in Babylon under the name *Sacaea*. Here, over the course of a five-day festival, every civil and social bond was sundered—but the center of it all was sexual licentiousness, the annihilation of all familiality through an unbounded hetaerism. The picture of the Greek celebration of Dionysus, as set down by Euripides in *The Bacchae*, offers the very counter-image; from it flows that same charm, the same musically transfiguring intoxication, that Skopas and Praxiteles concretized in statues. A messenger tells of being drawn up with the herds to the mountaintops in the midday heat; it is the right moment and the right place to see the hitherto unseen. Now, Pan sleeps; now, the heavens serve as dispassionate backdrop to a splendor; now, day b l o o m s .[13] The messenger marks three choruses of women upon an alpine meadow, lying dispersed and demurely composed upon the ground; many women are leaning against the trunks of firs—all are slumbering. Suddenly, the mother of Pentheus begins rejoicing; sleep is banished, all spring up, a model of noble customs; the girls and women let down their hair, locks falling on shoulders, and arrange their doeskins if the ribbons and bows have come undone while sleeping. They gird themselves with snakes, whose tongues lick intimately their cheeks, and several women take young wolves and deer up in arms and suckle them. All are adorned with garlands of ivy and morning glories; a blow of the *thyrsus* upon the rocks and water springs out, a rap with the rod upon the ground and a wine-spring rises up. Sweet honey drips from the branches; so much as touch the earth with fingertips, and snow-white milk bursts forth. —This is a wholly enchanted world; nature celebrates its festival of reconciliation with humans. The myth tells of Apollo putting back together once more the shattered Dionysus. This is the image of Dionysus created anew through Apollo, rescued from his Asiatic dismemberment. —

2.

In their perfect state,[14] such as we encounter them already in Homer, the Greek gods are certainly not to be conceived of as born of necessity and want. Certainly, the soul who quavers with dread never dreamt up such a mode of being [*Wesen*]; it was not in order to steer clear of life that an ingenious fantasy projected images of the gods upon the sky. A religion of life, not of duty or ascesis or ethereal spirituality, speaks out from these gods. All these figures breathe the triumph of existence; a luxurious feeling of living accompanies their cult. They do not order or demand: in them, what lies present at hand is deified, irrespective of whether it be good or evil. Measured against other religions' seriousness, holiness, and severity, the religion of the Greeks risks being undervalued as fantastical playing about [*Spielerei*]—if we do not call to mind an often unrecognized move of the deepest wisdom, through which that Epicurean being of the gods appears [*erscheint*] suddenly as the creation of a people artistic beyond compare, very nearly as the highest creation of all. It is the philosophy of the p e o p l e that the forest god in his chains reveals to mortals: "Best is not to be, second-best to die quickly."[15] It is this same philosophy that forms the background of the Greek pantheon. The Greeks knew well the horrors and outrages of existence, but cloaked them in order to go on living: a cross hidden beneath roses, in the symbol of Goethe. That luminous Olympian world came to dominance only because the grim administration of *moīra*, which determines for Achilles an early death and for Oedipus that loathsome marriage, is to be hidden by the radiant forms of Zeus, Apollo, Hermes, and so forth. Had someone stripped that i n t e r m e d i a r y   w o r l d of its artistic s e e m i n g [*künstlerischer S c h e i n*], they would have had to heed the wisdom of the forest god, the Dionysian companion. It was out of this adversity that the artistic genius of this people created their gods. For that reason, theodicy was never a Hellenic problem; they knew better than to attribute the existence[16] of the world—and therewith responsibility for its state—to the gods. Even the gods were submitted to *anānke*; this is an affirmation of the rarest wisdom. To see its existence as it actually is in a transfiguring mirror and to protect itself from the Medusa with this very mirror—this was the ingenious strategy pursued by the Hellenic "Will" in order to be able to live at all. For how else could such a people, so infinitely sensitive, so brilliant in their capacity for s   u   f   f   e   r   i   n   g ,   have borne existence i f   t h i s   i t s e l f   had not been revealed to them in their gods, engulfed in a greater glory! That same drive that called art to life as the supplement and perfection of existence, that tempts men into living on, also made possible the emergence of the Olympian world, a world of beauty [*Schönheit*], of tranquility, of enjoyment.

Through the operation of such a religion, life was grasped in the Homeric world as that which was in itself most worthy of struggle: life lived beneath the bright sunshine [*Sonnenschein*] of such gods. The p a i n of the Homeric man was bound to departure from this existence, above all to the nearness of that departure; when a complaint sounds out [*ertönt*] at all, it resounds for "short-lived Achilles," for the rapid changing of the human race, for the disappearing of the age of heroes. It is not unworthy of the greatest heroes to yearn to live on, even as day laborers. Never has the "Will" expressed itself more openly than in Hellenism, whose very complaint is still a hymn of praise. That's why modern man longs for this era in which he believes he hears a full attunement between nature and the human; that's why "Hellenic" is the term of salvation for all those who must seek out lustrous examples for their conscious affirmation of Will.[17] That's why, finally, the concept of "Greek cheerfulness" has arisen at the hands of hedonistic writers, such that a dilettantish life of leisure dares in disreputable fashion to excuse itself, even to honor itself, with the word "Greek."

In these conceptions, erring all, from the noblest to the meanest, Hellenism is taken too crudely and simply, formed more or less in the image of nations that lack ambiguity and are, so to speak, one-sided (for instance, the Romans). All the same, one must presume a need for artistic seeming [*künstlerisch Schein*] even in the vision of the world of a people that takes care to turn all it touches to gold. Actually, as already suggested, we also encounter an extraordinary illusion [*Illusion*] within this vision of the world, the same illusion of which nature so regularly avails itself in the attainment of its goals. The true aim is concealed by a hallucination; it is toward this that we stretch out our hands, reaching nature through this deception. In the Greeks, the Will would view itself transfigured as a work of art: in order to exalt itself, its own creation would have to feel itself worthy of being exalted, would have to re-envision itself lifted up to a higher sphere—lifted up into the realm of ideality, so to speak, without this perfect world of the vision functioning as imperative or reproach. This is the sphere of beauty [Schönheit], in which the Greeks catch sight of their mirror images, the Olympians. With this weapon, the Hellenic Will battled that talent correlative to the artistic, the talent for s u f f e r i n g and for the wisdom of suffering. Out of this battle and as a monument to victory, tragedy was born.

The i n t o x i c a t i o n o f s u f f e r i n g and t h e b e a u t i f u l d r e a m have their distinct pantheons. The first, in the omnipotence of its being, pierces the innermost thoughts of nature; it cognizes the fearsome drive toward existence and at once the continual dying of all that enters into existence. The gods it creates are good and evil, resembling chance; they horrify with sudden intentionality, are pitiless, and take no pleasure in the beautiful. They are akin to truth and approximate the concept [Begriff]; seldom do they coalesce into figures, and then with difficulty. To gaze upon them is to turn to stone; how should one live with them? But one should not—this is their lesson.

The gaze must be drawn away from this pantheon—if it cannot, like a criminal secret, be hidden entirely—drawn away by the luminous dream-birth of the Olympian world nearby. Hence does the blaze of Olympus' colors heighten, the sensuality of its figures grow ever greater, the more strongly truth or its symbol asserts itself. Never, however, was the struggle between truth and beauty greater than with the invasion of the Dionysian ritual; in this ritual, nature disclosed itself and spoke of its secret with terrible clarity, with that tone against which seductive seeming [*Schein*] nearly lost its sway. The spring flowed up in Asia, but in Greece it became a river; it had to, for here it found for the first time what Asia could not offer it: the most excitable sensibility and capacity for suffering, coupled with the lightest deliberateness and sharp-sightedness. How did Apollo save Hellenism? The newcomer was transported up into the world of beautiful seeming [*des schönen Scheins*], the world of Olympus; much of the honor of the most esteemed divinities, Zeus and Apollo, for example, was given over to him. Never has more trouble been taken for a stranger—and he was a fearsome stranger, too (*hostis* in every sense), powerful enough to smash the hospitable house to pieces. A great revolution began in all forms of life: everywhere, Dionysus burst in, even into art.

Beholding [*das Schauen*], the beautiful or seemly [*das Schöne*], what shines or seems [*Schein*][18]: these bound the realm of Apollonian art; it is the transfigured world of the eye that creates artistically, behind closed eyelids, in the dream. It is into this dream state that t h e   e p i c means to transport us; with open eyes, we should see nothing and feast on internal images—rhapsody seeks, through concepts, to incite us to the production of these images. The effects of the image-making arts are here arrived at via a detour; the image-maker leads us through hewn marble to the l i v i n g god he beholds in the dream—such that the figure swimming before him as authentic *tēlos* becomes clear as much for the image-maker as for the onlooker,

40

and the former gives the latter to follow along through the m e d i a t i n g f i g u r e of the statue. Meanwhile, the epic poet sees this same living figure and would also present it for the view of others, but he no longer places a statue between himself and humanity. Much more, he narrates how this figure demonstrates its life in movement, tone, word, action; he forces us to trace a host of effects back to their cause, requiring of us our own artistic composition.[19] He has achieved his aim when we see the figure or constellation or image clearly before us, when he has imparted to us that dreamlike state in which he himself first begat these presentations. That the epic demands of us a p l a s t i c creating shows how absolutely different lyric is from epic, since lyric never has as its aim the forming of images. The commonality between the two is merely something material, the word, or even more generally, the concept; if we speak of poetry, we do not thereby have some category wherein image-making art and music would be coordinated, but have rather an agglomeration of two art media entirely differentiated in themselves, of which the one connotes a path toward image-making art and the other a path to music. Both, however, are only paths toward the making of art, not arts themselves. In this sense, painting and sculpture too are naturally only art media; authentic art is the ability to make images [*Erschaffenkönnen von Bildern*], regardless of whether this be making-up [*Vor-schaffen*] or making-after [*Nach-schaffen*]. It is on this characteristic, a generally human one, that the c u l t u r a l s i g n i f i c a n c e of art is based. The artist—as the one who compels motion through art media toward art—cannot be simultaneously the absorptive instrument of art's own activity.

Apollonian c u l t u r e ' s idolatry, whether expressed in temples, statues, or the Homeric epic, had the ethical demand for measure as its sublime aim, which ran parallel to the aesthetic demand for beauty. To levy a demand for measure is only possible where there is measure, where the limit is c o g n i z a b l e . To be able to maintain one's boundaries, one must know them: hence the Apollonian dictum, *gnothi seautōn*. The mirror, however, in which the Apollonian Greek alone could see and thus cognize himself, was the Olympian pantheon; but here he apprehended his ownmost being [*sein eigenstes Wesen*] once more, shrouded in the beautiful seeming of the dream. Measure, under whose yoke the new pantheon labored (opposite the fallen world of the Titans), was the measure of beauty [*Schönheit*]; the limit within which the Greek had to hold himself was that of beautiful seeming [*des schönen Scheins*]. The innermost purpose of a culture oriented toward seeming [*Schein*] and measure can only be the veiling of truth: the tireless seekers in its service were hailed, just like the overthrown Titans, with the warning *medēn āgan*. In Prometheus, the Greeks were given an example of how too-great a care for human knowledge was ruinous for both the one who cared and those cared-for. He who in his wisdom would stand before the god must, like Hesiod, *mētron ēchein sophīes*.

It was into such a constructed and artistically protected [*künstlich geschützte*] world that the ecstatic tone of the Dionysian celebration penetrated. In this tone, nature's total i m m o d e r a t i o n was revealed: in pleasure, suffering, and cognition all at once. All that had thus far counted as limit, as measuring determination, proved itself here but artificial seeming [*künstlicher Schein*]; "immoderation" laid itself bare as the truth. For the first time, in complete drunkenness, the demonically fascinating song of the people trumpeted out an overpowering feeling. Against that feeling, what could the psalmodying artist of Apollo signify, with the only fearfully allusive strains of his *cithara*? What once had been jealously boxed and transplanted into the poetic-musical guild halls and simultaneously held at a distance from all profane participation, what had to be frozen with the force of the Apollonian genius to the level of a simple architectonics—the musical element— here cast off all constraints. Rhythmics, which before had moved in only the simplest of zigs and zags, now let loose its limbs in the Bacchanalian dance. T o n e sounded out, no longer as before with wraithlike thinness, but rather with the thousandfold intensification of the masses[20] and with the accompaniment of deep-toned wind instruments. And that greatest mystery of all transpired: harmony came here into the world, in its movement making the Will of nature immediately understood. Now, in Dionysus' surroundings, those things that had been secreted in art in the Apollonian world became clamorous; all the sheen of the Olympian gods dulled before the wisdom of Silenus. An art that spoke the truth in ecstatic intoxication banished the muses of the arts of seeming [*die Musen der Scheinkünste*]; in the self-forgottenness [*Selbstvergessenheit*] of the Dionysian state of being, the *individuum*—with its limits and measure—went under.[21] A twilight of the gods stood near at hand.

What was the intention of the Will, which is after all a singular o n e , in permitting the Dionysian elements to make inroads into its own Apollonian creation?

A new and higher *mēchanē* of existence had come into play, the birth of t r a g i c t h o u g h t . —

43

3.

The ecstasy of the Dionysian state, with its annihilation of existence's customary constraints and limits, includes throughout its duration a l e t h a r g i c element, in which all that is lived sinks down into the past. Through this gulf of forgottenness, the worlds of quotidian and Dionysian actuality separate from one another. As soon as that quotidian actuality once more enters into consciousness, it is felt as such with d i s g u s t [*Ekel*]: an a s c e t i c , Will-denying disposition[22] is the fruit of these conditions. In thought, the Dionysian is set up as a higher ordering of the world, opposite something common and base; the Greek wanted total flight from this world of guilt and fate. He did not comfort himself with a world after death; his longing rose higher, over and above the gods, denying existence all its brightly gleaming mirroring of the gods. In the consciousness of coming to from intoxication, he sees everywhere the awfulness and absurdity of human being—it disgusts him. Now, he understands the wisdom of the forest-god.

Here we arrive at the most dangerous limit that the Hellenic Will, with its Apollonian-optimistic founding principle, could tolerate. Here, the Hellenic Will set to work immediately with its natural healing power, reversing that negating disposition; its means are the tragic work of art and the tragic idea. Its intent absolutely could not be to weaken, still less to suppress, the Dionysian state; direct coercion was impossible and, if it was possible, far too dangerous—for, if detained in its outpouring, the element would then break for itself some other course and infuse all the veins of life.

Above all, that disgusted thought of the awfulness and the absurdity of existence had to be transformed into presentations with which one could live: these are the s u b l i m e as the artistic taming of the awful and the r i d i c u l o u s as the artistic discharge of disgust at the absurd. These two intertwining elements are unified in a work of art that imitates intoxication, that plays with intoxication.

The sublime and the ridiculous go a step beyond the world of beautiful seeming, for in both concepts there is sensed a contradiction. On the other hand, in no way do these coincide with truth; they are the veiling of the truth, more transparent than beauty, it is true, but a veiling all the same. In them, therefore, we have an i n t e r m e d i a r y world between beauty and truth; here, a unification of Dionysus and Apollo is possible. This world reveals itself in play with intoxication, not in being wholly caught up in it. In the actor [*Schauspieler*],[23] we apprehend once more the Dionysian man, the instinctive poet singer dancer, but now as a p l a y - a c t e d Dionysian man. He seeks to attain to his model in the convulsions of sublimity or else in the convulsions of laughter; he transcends beauty and yet he does not seek truth. He remains floating in between the two. He strives not for beautiful seeming [*nach dem schönen Schein*], but for seeming [*nach dem Schein*] nonetheless; not for truth [*nach der Wahrheit*], but for the s e e m i n g o f t r u t h [*nach Wahrscheinlichkeit*].[24] (Symbol, sign of truth.) Initially, of course, the actor was not a solitary individual; the Dionysian mass, the people, was meant to be represented—hence, the dithyrambic chorus. Through play with intoxication, the actor, along with the surrounding chorus of onlookers [*Zuschauer*], was meant to be more or less relieved of intoxication. From the standpoint of the Apollonian world, Hellenism needed to be h e a l e d and e x p i a t e d ; Apollo, the proper god of healing and expiation, rescued the Greeks from c l e a r -eyed ecstasy and disgust at existence—through the artwork of tragic-comedic thought.

The new world of art, the world of the sublime and the ridiculous, of "the seeming of truth" [*Wahrscheinlichkeit*], was concerned with another vision of the gods and of the world than was that older one of beautiful seeming [*des schönen Scheins*]. Cognition the horrors and absurdities of existence, the deranged order of things—plan-like but without reason—altogether, the most monstrous s u f f e r i n g in all of nature unveiled the artfully cloaked figures of *moīra* and the Erinyes, of Medusa and the Gorgon; the Olympian gods were in the gravest danger. In tragic-comic works of art, they were saved by being themselves plunged into the sea of the sublime and the ridiculous; they ceased to be merely "beautiful," and absorbed into themselves, so to speak, that older order of gods and their sublimity. Now, they split into two groups, with but few floating in between: as sometimes sublime, sometimes ridiculous divinities. Above all, Dionysus himself was accorded this bifurcated form of being.

Now, in the tragic period of Hellenism, two characters best display how it again became possible to live: Aeschylus and Sophocles. The sublime appears [*erscheint*] to Aeschylus, as a thinker, most often in the most extraordinary justice. For him, Man and god share the tightest subjective commonality: the divine just ethical[25] and the h a p p y[26] are uniformly entwined with one another. It is on these scales that the individual being, whether man or Titan, is measured. The gods were reconstructed according to this norm of justice. So, for example, the folk belief in a demon who blinded and tempted people to guilt—a remnant of that primordial pantheon dethroned by the Olympians—was corrected, making of this demon a tool in the hands of a justly punishing Zeus. The equally primordial—likewise foreign to the Olympians—thought of a family curse was stripped of all bitterness, since with Aeschylus there is no n e e d for individual wickedness and everyone can escape the curse.

While Aeschylus finds the sublime in the sublimity of the Olympian administration of justice, Sophocles sees this—in wondrous fashion—in the sublimity of the imperviousness of the Olympian administration of justice. He recovers the folk standpoint at every point. The undeservedness of an awful fate seemed to him sublime; the truly insoluble puzzles of human existence were his tragic muse. With him, Suffering attains its transfiguration; it is conceived of as something sanctifying. The distance between the human and the divine is immeasurable; accordingly, the most profound submission and resignation are fitting. The proper virtue is *sophrosyne*, properly a negative virtue. Heroic humanity is the costliest humanity without this virtue; its fate demonstrates this infinite divide. There is scarcely such a thing as g u i l t , only a lack of cognition concerning the value of the human and its limits.

This standpoint is certainly deeper and more intrinsic than that of Aeschylus, coming close to signifying the Dionysian truth and expressing it without many symbols—and yet! we apprehend here the ethical principle of Apollo braided into the Dionysian vision of the world. With Aeschylus, disgust is dissolved in the sublime shudder at the wisdom of the ordering of the world, which is d i f f i c u l t to cognize only because of human weakness. With Sophocles, this shudder is grander still, because that wisdom is wholly unfathomable. This is the pure voice of piety, which is without struggle, whereas Aeschylus continually has the task of justifying the divine administration of justice and, for that reason, always remains standing before new problems. The "limit of the human," which Apollo ordered examined, is for Sophocles cognizable, but is narrower and more constrained than was meant in the pre-Dionysian era of Apollo. Human lack of self-knowledge is the Sophoclean problem, human lack of knowledge of the gods, the Aeschylian.

Piety, most wondrous mask of the life-drive! Dedication to a perfected d r e a m - w o r l d , to be awarded by the highest ethical w i s d o m ! Flight from truth, the better to worship it from afar, shrouded in clouds! Reconciliation with actuality, b e c a u s e it is an enigma! Repulsion by unriddling, because we are no gods! Lustful prostration in the dirt, contentment [*Glücksruhe*] in ill fortune [*Unglück*]! Highest *kenosis* of humanity in its highest expression! Glorification and transfiguration of existence's media of horror and terrifyingness as the very cure for existence! Joyful living in the denigration of life! Triumph of the Will in its negation!

At this stage of cognition there are only two paths: that of the saint and that of the t r a g i c a r t i s t .[27] Both have in common that they can live on [*fortleben*] with the clearest cognition of the nullity of existence, without feeling a rift in their vision of the world. Disgust at still living [*Weiterleben*] is taken as the means of creation, whether this be saintly or artistic. The horrible or the absurd is uplifting, because it is only seemingly [*scheinbar*] horrible or absurd. The Dionysian power of enchantment here proves itself, even at the highest point of this vision of the world; all that is actual gives way to seeming [*Schein*] and behind it is announced the u n i t a r y   n a t u r e   o f   t h e   W i l l , wholly wrapped in the glory of wisdom and truth, in dazzling brilliance. I l l u s i o n,   d e l u s i o n i s a t i ts p e a k . —

Now, it will no longer be thought incomprehensible that the very same Will that, as Apollonian, ordered the Hellenic world came to incorporate its other manifestation [*Erscheinungsform*], the Dionysian Will. The struggle between these two manifestations of Will had an extraordinary aim: to create a h i g h e r   p o s s i b i l i t y   o f e x i s t e n c e and, also, to arrive in this at a still h i g h e r   g l o r i f i c a t i o n (through art). No longer the art of seeming [*Kunst des Scheins*], but rather tragic art was the form of this glorification; in it, however, that art of seeming is entirely absorbed. Apollo and Dionysus have merged. Just as the Dionysian element infiltrated Apollonian life, as seeming [*Schein*] established itself as limit even here, so, too, is Dionysian-tragic art no longer "truth." No longer is this singing and dancing instinctive, natural intoxication; no longer is the mass of the chorus, Dionysically frenzied, the mass of the people, gripped unconsciously by the drive of spring. Truth is now s y m b o l i z e d . It avails itself of seeming, and therefore can and must also make use of the arts of seeming. Already, however, a great difference from earlier art shows itself. Now, all of seeming's artistic media [*Kunstmittel des Scheines*] are c o l l e c t i v e l y   b r o u g h t   t o   b e a r and, furthermore, the statue is transformed, the paintings of the *periactoi* shifted; one and the same rear wall is presented to the eye now as a temple, now as a palace. We note also at the same time a certain i n d i f f e r e n c e   t o w a r d   s e e m i n g [*Schein*], which must now surrender its immortal claims, its sovereign demands. Seeming is no longer enjoyed at all as s e e m i n g , but rather as   s y m b o l , as sign of truth. Hence the consolidation—inherently offensive—of artistic media. The clearest evidence of this disdain for seeming is the   m a s k .

The Dionysian demand is thus made of the onlooker: that he imagine everything enchanted, that he see always more than the symbol, that the entire visible world of the scene and orchestra be the r e a l m   o f   w o n d e r m e n t . But where is the force that will transport him into this disposition of belief in miracles, through which he will see all as enchanted? Who vanquishes the force of seeming and relegates it to symbol? This is   m u s i c . —

4.

Philosophy in the Schopenhauerian vein teaches us to conceive of what we term "feeling" as a complex of unconscious presentations [*Vorstellungen*] and states of Will [*Willenszuständen*]. The Will's aspirations, however, communicate themselves only as pleasure or displeasure and therein as merely quantitative differentiation. There are no species of pleasure, though there are certainly degrees and a welter of accompanying presentations. We must understand pleasure as gratification of the o n e   Will, displeasure as its non-gratification.

In what manner, then, does feeling impart itself? Partially, but only very partially, it can be transposed into thoughts, that is, into conscious presentations; obviously, this only holds for a portion of the accompanying presentations. There always remains in this area of feeling, however, an indissoluble remainder. Language, that is, the concept, is concerned solely with what is soluble; henceforth, the limit of " p o e t r y " is determined by the feeling's capacity for expression.

The other two sorts of imparting are instinctive through and through, without consciousness and yet functionally purposive. These are the languages of g e s t u r e and of t o n e . The language of gesture is comprised of generally understandable symbols and is produced through reflex movements. These symbols are visible: the eye that sees them immediately imparts the circumstances that engendered the gesture which they symbolize; for the most part, the one who sees feels a sympathetic innervation of the same parts of the face or limbs that it perceives.[28] Symbol signifies here a quite imperfect, piecemeal likeness, an allusive sign, the particular understanding of which stands to be negotiated; it is only that in this case, the understanding common to all is i n s t i n c t i v e , that is, it has not passed through the light of consciousness.

W h a t , then, does g e s t u r e symbolize of that dualistic being [*Doppelwesen*], of feeling?

Clearly, it is the a c c o m p a n y i n g p r e s e n t a t i o n , since only this can be alluded to through visible gesticulation, imperfectly and piecemeal: an image can only be symbolized by an image.[29]

Painting and sculpture represent humans in the gesture, that is, they imitate the symbol and achieve their effects when we understand that symbol. The pleasure of viewing [Anschauen] consists in understanding the symbol despite its appearance [Schein].

The actor [Schauspieler], by contrast, represents the symbol in actuality, not merely in appearance [zum Scheine]; yet his effect on us does not arise from our understanding of this symbol. Much more, we plunge into the symbolized feeling and no longer tarry with our pleasure in appearances [Lust am Schein], with beautiful seeming [schönen Schein].

Thus, the scenery in drama does not arouse the pleasure of seeming [Lust des Scheins] in the least; rather, we grasp it as a symbol and understand the actuality alluded to therewith. Mannequins and actual plants are, alongside clearly painted ones, entirely admissible as evidence that here we make present actuality [Wirklichkeit], not artistic seeming [kunstvoller Schein]. Likelihood, or the seeming of truth [Wahrscheinlichkeit]—and no longer beauty [Schönheit]—is here the task.

But what is beauty? — "The rose is beautiful" means only: the rose has a nice appearance [hat einen guten Schein]; it has something appealingly luminous about it. Nothing about its essence is meant to be communicated thereby. It appeals, it awakens pleasure as seeming [Schein]: that is, through its appearing [Scheinen], the Will is gratified; pleasure in existence is fostered therein. The rose is— according to its appearance [Schein]—a faithful likeness of its Will; or, identical to this formulation, in its seeming [Schein], it corresponds to the definition of the genus.

The better it does so, the more beautiful [it][30] is; if in its very being it corresponds to that definition, then it is "good."

"A beautiful painting" signifies only this: the notion that we have of a painting is here accomplished. When, however, we call a painting "good," then we designate our notion of a painting as that which accords with the e s s e n c e of this painting. For the most part, however, what is understood as beautiful is a painting that represents something beautiful; this is the judgment of laypeople. They enjoy the beauty of the material, and j u s t   s o   are we to enjoy the image-making arts in drama, except that here the task cannot be to represent only what is beautiful: it is enough if it seems t r u e [scheint wahr]. The object represented should be conceived of in as sensually alive a fashion as possible; it should function as truth—a requirement whose o p p o s i t e is claimed for every work of beautiful seeming [des schönen Scheins]. —

If, however, the gesture symbolizes the presentation accompanying a feeling, by what symbol are the stirrings of the W i l l itself to understanding to be i m p a r t e d ? Which is here the instinctive mediation?

The m e d i a t i o n o f t o n e . More precisely, it is the various manners of pleasure and displeasure—absent every accompanying presentation [begleitende Vorstellung]—that tone symbolizes.

All that we could claim to be characteristic of the various sensations of displeasure are images of the presentations that become legible through the symbolism of gesture—as, for example, when we speak of a sudden shock, of the "throbbing, straining, wincing, sticking tearing biting thrill" of pain.[31] With this, certain of the Will's "forms of intermittence" seem to be revealed: put briefly—in the symbolism of the language of tone— r h y t h m i c s . We cognize once more, in the d y n a m i c s of tone, the plenitude of the intensifications of the Will, the alternating quantity of pleasure and displeasure. But the proper being of the Will takes refuge in h a r m o n y, not allowing itself to be expressed by comparison. The Will and its symbol—harmony—both p u r e l o g i c at base! While rhythmics and dynamics are up to a point still the exterior of a Will that is announced in symbols, indeed, are nearly the model of appearances as such [*Erscheinung an sich*], harmony is the symbol of the pure essence of the Will. In rhythmics and dynamics, accordingly, the individual phenomenon [*Einzelerscheinung*] is still to be characterized as an appearance [*Erscheinung*]; it is from this side that music can be developed as the art of seeming [*Kunst des Scheins*]. Harmony, the indissoluble remainder, speaks of the Will within and without all manifestations [*Erscheinungsformen*] and is, therefore, not merely a s y m b o l i s m of feeling but rather o f t h e w o r l d . In i t s sphere, the concept is entirely powerless.[32]

Now we comprehend the significance of the language of gesture and the language of tone f o r t h e D i o n y s i a n a r t w o r k . In the people's primitive spring-dithyramb, man would express himself not as *individuum*, but as species-man. That he ceases to be an individual man is revealed through the symbolism of the eye, expressed in the language of gesture such that he speaks as a s a t y r , as natural being among natural beings, in gestures and, indeed, in the intensified language of gesture, in g e s t u r e s   o f   d a n c e . Through tone, however, he expresses the innermost thoughts of nature; it is not only as the genius of the species, as in g e s t u r e , but as the genius of existence in itself that the Will here makes itself immediately understandable. With gesture, then, the Will remains within the boundaries of the species, that is, in the world of appearances [*Erscheinungswelt*], but with tone it dissolves the world of the appearance [*Welt der Erscheinung*], so to speak, into its originary unity; the world of the Maya disappears before its enchantment.

But when does natural man come to the symbolism of tone? When does the language of gesture no longer suffice? When does tone become music? Above all, in the Will's highest states of pleasure and displeasure, as exultant Will or when frightened to death; in short, in the i n t o x i c a t i o n   o f   f e e l i n g : in the   s c r e a m .[33] How much more powerful and immediate is the scream than the gaze! But even the milder excitations of the will have their tonal symbolism; in general, a tone is parallel to every gesture— to intensify the tone to pure sound falls to the intoxication of feeling alone.

It is the most intimate and common mixture of a sort of gestural symbolism and tone that we call l a n g u a g e .[34] In the word, through tone and case, the emphasis and rhythm of its sound, the essence of the thing [*Wesen des Dinges*] is symbolized; through the gesture of the mouth, the accompanying presentation, the image, the appearance of the essence [*Erscheinung des Wesens*]. Symbols can and must be multiple; they develop, however, instinctively and with great and wise regularity. An apprehended symbol is a   c o n c e p t : since in being

55

detained in memory the tone fades entirely away, in the concept only the symbol of the accompanying presentation is retained. That which one can designate and differentiate, one has "grasped."

In the intensification of feeling, the essence of the word reveals itself more clearly and sensually in the symbol of tone [*Ton*]; this is why it resounds [*tönt*] more.[35] *Sprechgesang* is more or less a return to nature: the symbol that has become deadened in the course of use regains its originary power.

In the arrangement of words, that is, through a chain of symbols, something new and grander is to be symbolically represented; in this capacity, rhythmics, dynamics, and harmony once more become necessary. This wider circle now rules over the more narrow one of the individual word; words must be elected, newly positioned—poetry begins. The operatic recitation of a sentence is not some sort of succession of word-sounds, for a word has only a very relative sound, since its essence, its content as represented by the symbol, varies depending on its positioning. In other words, out of the higher unity of the sentence and the essence symbolized through it, the individual symbol of the word is perpetually determined anew. A chain of concepts is a thought; this is, then, the higher unity of the accompanying presentations. The essence of the thing is out of thought's reach—that it nonetheless works upon us as a motive, as an excitation of the Will, is explicable by the fact that the thought is already an apprehended symbol for a phenomenon of Will [*Willenserscheinung*], for the stirring and the appearance of the Will [*Erscheinung des Willens*] all at once. It is as spoken, however, that is, with the symbolism of tone, that the Will works to incomparably greater and more direct effect. Sung—there it attains the high-point of its effectivity, as long as the *melos* is the understandable symbol of its Will; when this is not the case, the sequence of tones and the arrangement of words affect us, but the thought remains distant, a matter of indifference.

Depending on whether the word is to work primarily as symbol of the accompanying presentation or as symbol of the originary stirring of the Will, whether therefore images or feelings are to be symbolized, two paths of poetry diverge: the epic and the lyric. The former leads to image-making or visual art, the latter to music; pleasure in appearances [*Lust an der Erscheinung*] rules over the epic, while the Will reveals itself in the lyric. That cuts loose from music, this remains in league with it.

In the Dionysian dithyramb, however, the Dionysian fanatic[36] is incited to the highest intensification of his symbolic capacity—something never-yet felt presses for expression: the annihilation of the *individuatio*, one-being [*Einssein*] in the genius of the species, indeed, nature itself. Now, the essence of nature seeks expression. A new world of symbols is necessary; the accompanying presentations become symbols in images of an intensified human essence, represented with the greatest psychic energy through that entirely corporeal symbolism, through gestural dance. But the world of the Will, too, demands an unheard-of symbolic expression: the forces of harmony of dynamics of rhythmics grow suddenly tumultuous. Divided between the two worlds, poetry too requires a new sphere—at once the sensuality of the image, as in epic, and tone's intoxication of feeling, as in lyric. To apprehend this total unleashing of all the symbolic powers is the

57

purview of that very intensification of essence that brought it about; the dithyrambic servant of Dionysus will only be understood by his peers. That's why this whole new world of art, in all its wildly foreign, seductive wondrousness, rolls through Apollonian Hellenism only with fearsome s t r u g g l e s .

Translator's Notes

1. The *Weltanschauung* of Nietzsche's title is at once more and less than a "world-view" or "vision of the world." Where these suggest something on the order of a conscious idea and theory of the world—what we, in more thinking times, were wont to call a philosophy—a *Weltanschauung* both precedes and encompasses all conscious philosophies. As a vision of things more or less particular to a subject and prior to all conscious thought, *Anschauung* has, since Kant, typically been rendered in English as "intuition," underscoring its relative interiority but also the sense in which it is perceptive of some external world. The difficulty with "intuition," however, is that it loses the visuality, the "viewing," "on-looking," or "looking-at" of the verb *anschauen*. One of the best, and oldest, discussions of the difficulties in translating Kant's *Anschauung* is to be found in Edward Hegeler's 1882 "What does Anschauung Mean," in *The Monist*. In apprehending Nietzsche's *Weltanschauung* here as a "vision of the world," the reader should keep in mind that what is at stake is a way of apprehending, of perceiving the world; this is a perceptual function by which perceiving subjects are themselves constituted. Acordingly, the "vision" in question should not be confused with a romantic fancy, as in the children's rhyme in which "visions of sugar-plums danced in their heads." To the contrary, the *Weltanschauung* is a primary way of seeing, a vision of the world that makes a world cohere, come into focus for a subject. It is to be contrasted with the *Begriff* or "concept," which is produced by conscious subjects as a separate act of intellection (see n35 *sub*).

2. Although "existence" is a common enough translation of *Dasein*, there is value—especially given the mixed history of its renderings in both English and French after Heidegger—in considering a little more carefully the original. *Dasein*, literally, "there-being" or "being-there," was crucially, for Hegel, "determinate being" as such: being determined simply *as* being without yet being something in particular (*Dasein* logically preceding *Etwas*). As Stephen Houlgate notes, "before all else determinate being is the *settled* unity of being and nothing"; as this settled unity, it is opposed to becoming, "the restless vanishing of being and nothing into one another" (2006, 300). *Dasein* in Hegel's

Logic, then, is the basic character or quality of existence (as we comprehend it), the speculative unity of being and nothing (in our understanding). Meanwhile, for Schiller in *Über die ästhetische Erziehung des Menschen*, *Dasein* is the naturally determinate character of being over and above all speculative comprehension—*Dasein* is natural being in itself, quite apart from the play of *Schein* or seeming that is the essential mark of human visions of the world. *Dasein* for Nietzsche refers much more to the particular manner of being that does the understanding; it is that being over and above the understanding of being that makes understanding possible—not simply a category of thought or a natural kind, it is here a "blissful feeling." This is already much more the *Dasein* we will see subsequently in Heidegger: the *ek-stasis* particular to a certain sort of being, a kind of being that is certainly not the rationally conscious human subject (hence the difficulty with Henri Corbin's early translation of *Dasein* into French as *la réalité humaine*), but is at once more specific and particular than Hegel's resolutely general "determinate being" and more specifically human than Schiller's natural being. *Dasein* is for Nietzsche, as subsequently for Heidegger, "existence" in the sense that human beings "exist," being the ecstatic mediation between subject-being and object-being. It is notable that *Rausch*, the "intoxication" wherein existence is feelingly achieved, admits also of "ecstasy," "frenzy," and "rapture" as its translations.

3. Throughout, Nietzsche relies heavily on the different resonances of *scheinen*, at once "to seem" or "appear" and "to shine" or "glisten." *Schein* is multivalent in German: a "flash" or "glow" or even a "luster," an "appearance" or "pretense," and a "certificate" or "bill of proof" to boot. I have rendered it here with "seeming," as, on the whole, *Schein*'s brilliance is secondary—even compensatory—to its being apparent. At the same time, however, as Friedrich Ulfers notes in his introduction to this text, it is a mistake to think of *Schein* as "only apparent," as though there would be hidden behind all appearances some fuller reality—Nietzsche rejects the classical philosophical couplet of appearances and reality, offering us both a primordial "seeming" that is a semblance *of* truth (the semblance belonging to truth, rather than an illusion behind which stands the truth) and a secondary "seeming" that is constructed, an artificial (*kunstvoll*) illusion that makes life liveable. As in "On Truth and Lies in an Extramoral Sense," what is finally real is precisely the coming-to-be and the fading-away of appearances: the actual as such, here, the "fluttering veil of seeming." A non-pejorative "semblance" or "illusion" would thus be two other possibilities for *Schein*, but both have the disadvantage of straying from the accompanying cluster of terms: to seem (*scheinen*) and seemliness (*Schönheit*, typically translated as "beauty"), on the one hand, to appear (*scheinen* or *erscheinen*) and appearance or phenomenon (*Erscheinung*) on the other, with seemingly true or probable (*wahrscheinlich*) nearby—to say nothing of *schauen* and *anschauen* (to look or watch or gaze or view) and their various cousins. Herder notes of this cluster, so important for the German idealist aesthetics with which Nietzsche broke, that "*Schönheit* (beauty) takes its name from *Schauen* (looking) and from

Schein (seeming)" (*Sämtliche Werke*, VIII, 10; compare also "Does Painting or Music Have a Greater Effect? A Divine Colloquy," trans. Gregory Moore, 2006). The *scheinen*-cluster, unfortunately, does not find ready expression in English; I have offered some indication of its ubiquity by presenting the German in-text at particularly pertinent points.

4. *Vorstellung* was long rendered in philosophical writings as "representation," due in no small measure to this being the choice made both in earlier translations of Kant's *Critique of Judgment* and for Schopenhauer's *The World as Will and Representation*. This was happily amended to "presentation" in Werner Pluhar's 1987 translation of Kant, and Richard Acquila and David Carus have followed suit in a 2007/2010 freshening-up of Schopenhauer. As a verb, *vorstellen* indicates placement-before—implicitly before some viewer or subject, even if that subject be oneself. Accordingly, *Vorstellungen*, sometimes also translated as "ideas" or "mental representations," are those *qualia* placed before some receiver within that receiver him or herself; the term carries in it that sense in which one is a subject only by virtue of being acted not only *upon*, but also *in*, by an external world

5. The German term for prophesying, *wahrsagend*, is constructed from *wahr* and *sagen*—literally, "true-saying," truth-telling. Throughout this essay, *Wahrheit* (truth) remains in tension with *Schein* (seeming) and with the cluster of terms surrounding *Kunst* (art or artifice); for the latter, German follows the Greek τέχνη in maintaining an affinity between arts and crafts that, in English, survives only at farmers' markets.

6. With this "sonnenhaft"--"sunnily" or "sun-like"--Nietzsche seems to be quoting from Goethe's *Farbenlehre*. Speaking of a world in which "all nature reveals itself through color to the eye's sense" (1810, xxxvii), Goethe urges his reader to "remember the old Ionian school, which always reiterated with such great emphasis: only by like may like be known," and offers as well the verses of "an old mystic":

Were not the eye sun-like,
How should we behold the light?
Did not god's own power live within us,
How should the godly so delight us? (xxxviii)

7. *Allgemein*, literally "common to all," is often rendered in English with the Latinate "universal"; but the idea of the universal is summarily unitary, stipulating a totality that includes everything within it, whereas *allgemein* is constructively multiple—common to all, but immanent: not situated conceptually over and above that "all" as is a universe. I have typically presented *allgemein* with reference to the common.

8. *Weltenharmonie*, which also carries in itself the sense of "the harmony of worlding," since the noun *Welt* (world) is not only pluralized, but also potentially verbed by the addition of *–en*. As "the harmony of worlds" or even "music of the spheres" or "celestial harmony," Nietzsche's gospel of *Weltenharmonie* partakes in a long history of declarations of this good news. In the *Metaphysics*, Aristotle ascribes a vision of celestial harmony to the Pythagoreans, and the classical Daoist texts of Zhuangzi tell a similar tale, to name just two instances.

9. *Ton* is both "clay," as here, and "tone" or "sound" (from τόνος), as subsequently throughout the essay; nature's amanuensis, the Dionysian artist molds the human clay by means of musical tones

10. In the MU´SICA entry of their *Dictionary of Greek and Roman Antiquities*, William Smith, William Wayte, and G.E. Marindin observe that the Greek τόνος, "lit. 'tension,' 'pitch,' has two distinct special senses. It is applied to the keys, as being scales which differed in pitch. It is also the name of an interval, a tone; perhaps as being the interval through which the voice is most naturally raised at one effort" (1890, n1). Liddell and Scott's *Lexicon* has as a covering definition for τόν-ος, "that by which a thing is stretched, or that which can itself be stretched"; the various musical senses of the term are developed by this notion of stretching, a fact made entirely clear when one considers the phonetic effect of the tonos as a diacritical mark (1940). Nietzsche's discussion of tone must be read with this collection of resonances in mind

11. Equally, "from himself" or "out of himself."

12. *Lust* and *Unlust*, "pleasure" and "displeasure" respectively, harbor also that sense of "lust" that, in English, is indissociable from desire (not least, but not always directly, sexual desire). So, for example, *Lust auf's Leben* is at once "pleasure in living" and the more familiar "lust for life."

13. Compare with Hölderlin's promised blooming of the Grecian day in "Der Archipelagus":

> Until, wakened from anxious dream, the soul rises up
> From men, youthfully joyous, and the breath that blesses with love
> Once more, as oft before, among Hellas' blossoming children
> Shall waft in a new era and blow upon freer brows
> The spirit of nature, the far-roaming, once more to us
> Silently abiding in golden clouds, the god appear. (247 ff.)

14. *Vollendung*, which relies for conceptual coherence on the very possibility of being *voll endet*, brought fully to an end, entails a sense of perfection as completion that retains in its semantic motion the Aristotelian *tēlos*. As in Plato (see, for instance, the discussion at 346a-352e in *The Republic*), for Aristotle,

any thing in the world approaches its proper end or *tēlos* as a matter of its very nature or function, its *ergon*. To follow Nietzsche here, it is crucial to think, like the Greeks themselves, perfection and completion together.

15. Nietzsche here references Silenus, a demigod of sorts and wisest, most drunken companion of Dionysus; Plutarch reports that in the *Eudemus*, one of the lost works, Aristotle ascribed this particular piece of wisdom to Silenus. Plutarch, *Moralia*, "Consolation to Appollonius," 115b-e (179) and Cicero, *Tusculan Disputations* I.48 (114).

16. *Existenz*, here (as opposed to *Dasein* in all other instances), is the simple fact of being as such, much closer to Hegel's *Dasein* than to Heidegger's or Nietzsche's (or to Jaspers' *Existenz*); existence in this broadest possible sense marks the structural fact of being, as opposed to the more narrow—but for that rich—sense of existence offered up by human *Dasein*.

17. It bears mention that what will later be two of Nietzsche's most crucial concepts, *Lebensbejahung* ("affirmation of life") and *Wille zur Macht* ("will to power"), are here, from the very earliest moment, contained in a single term: *Willensbejahung*, or "affirmation of will." "Affirmation of will," however, presents a certain ambiguity, as does Nietzsche's repeated placement of the will within quotation marks. Is the will to be affirmed an individuated will to power—directly counterposed in *Zarathustra* to Schopenhauer's *Wille zum Leben* or "will to [one's own] life," and the "essence" of any life which could be affirmed? Or is the will to be affirmed here more on the order of a world- or culture-willing, as suggested when Nietzsche speaks in this essay of the "Hellenic Will"? Much hinges, not only for interpretation of *The Dionysian Vision of the World* and *The Birth of Tragedy*, but for Nietzsche's entire oeuvre, on whether one reads "will" as an individuated phenomenon, a panpsychic occurring, or both.

18. See viz. Herder's suggestion, cited n3 *supra*.

19. Compare with Hegel, who begins a section of the *Aesthetics*, Vol. III on "'The Reading and Reading Aloud of Dramatic Works" by observing that "the actual, sensual material of dramatic poetry is … not merely the human voice and the spoken word, but rather the whole human" (1971, 291). Arguing against a developing tendency among the Germans—to see epic poetry as something merely to be read, not actually staged—Hegel invokes the Greek tragedians as exemplary in their manner of creating for an audience that would itself be caught up in the living movement and action of *character* beyond all reflection. Importantly, however, where the Hegelian audience would be carried along by the actors, the Nietzschean audience must co-create for itself the very life-source of the living figures in which it is to delight.

63

20. Nietzsche is here playing on the homophony of *Maße*, the plural of "measure," and *Masse*, the singular-plural and awakening "masses." The masses now lend their voice to folk-songs, and in so doing not only overstep all bounds and measure but also increase and intensify all measuring. Nature is not characterized here by a "lack of measure," is not *ohne Maß*, but by "immoderation"; it is an *Übermaß*, a measuring that exceeds all measure, a thousandfold intensification of measure in the lifted voice of the masses.

21. The relation between *Selbstvergessenheit* (self-forgottenness), *Übermaß* (immoderation), and *Untergang* (going-under) in the dissolving of the *principium individuationis* runs a direct course from *The Dionysian Vision of the World* to *Thus Spoke Zarathustra*. Compare viz. the prologue of *Zarathustra*: "I love him whose soul is overfull, so that he forgets himself, and all things are in him: thus all things become his going under" (2005, 14).

22. Especially after Heidegger, *Stimmung* can be difficult to translate. Constructed from voice, or *Stimme*, in its ongoing determinative [*bestimmend*] character, we could go so far as to render *Stimmung* as "voicing," but this would be a fidelity to origins that loses track of the ongoing motion of language and also of the quasi-environmental character of *Stimmung*. I here render it primarily as "disposition," but urge the reader to bear in mind a sense of the simultaneously voicing, determining, and voiced force of any given disposition. "Mood," the general consensus for Heidegger's *Stimmung*, would be to read too much of Nietzsche's most famous reader back into Nietzsche himself.

23. The *Schauspieler* or actor—a "player" in the older English sense, as in Shakespeare's "All the world's a stage,/ And all the men and women merely players"—is one who plays, *spielt*, for the viewing, *schauen*, of others. In reading Nietzsche's discussions here of *Spiel* or "play," it is useful to keep in mind a Schillerian understanding of the human as an animal that plays: "What, however, does mere play mean, once we know that, in all human circumstances, it is precisely and only play that makes the human complete and unfolds at once his dual nature?" (1875, 240). The tragic player, with this in mind, is not merely an actor in the vulgar sense, a person who performs a role with some effects, but is one who plays out her ownmost being for show, for the viewing of others. Play, as Colli and Montinari observe in their endnotes to *KSA* I, comes specifically to signify "the activity of the actor [*Schauspieler*], unifying the two domains of experience": the Apollonian clarity of the dream and the Dionysian truth of intoxication (914). In playing with and playing out these two domains, the actor or player mediates in dreamlike Apollonian fashion the intoxicating Dionysian experience.

24. In *Wahrscheinlichkeit* (usually "probability" or "likelihood," here "the seeming of truth") concepts we take for granted as independent—probability, likelihood—are explicitly given as functions of a reality/appearance or

truth/seeming divide. In opposing the *wahrscheinlich* and the substantivized *Wahrscheinlichkeit* to what is *wahr*, the truth or *Wahrheit*, German takes up a Latin insight in a manner lost somewhat to English, except in our much constrained "verisimilitude." Compare, for instance, Cicero's description of the aims of rhetoric in *De inventione*: "Inventio est excogitatio rerum verarum aut veri similium quae causam probabilem reddant"; "Invention is discovery of or thinking-upon such *rerum verarum* or *rerum veri semilium*—such true things or things that are like unto truth, that seem true or resemble truth—as will render one's cause probable or plausible" (I.VII.9). It is this set of dependent oppositions that we must keep in mind when reading Nietzsche's *Wahrscheinlichkeit*, which might also be thought as something like "the tendency of seeming true."

25. Here, as with the comma-free "instinctive poet singer dancer" *supra*, or "nearly the temple nearly the palace" and "the forces of harmony of dynamics of rhythmics" *sub*, Nietzsche offers a metonymic chain of rising equivalences; "divine," "just," and "ethical" all are presented together by a single article, but each both amplifies and modifies its predecessor, which it also negates and proceeds from. It is not implausible to read these moments as expressions of a sort of *dialectique sauvage*.

26. In this connection, it is useful to consider the Moirai in their role as figures of fate; typically present in English simply as "the Fates," Clotho, Lachesis, and Atropos are invoked by Aeschylus sometimes as abstract figures, sometimes as personified and negotiating gods, but in Sophocles they are nearly always impersonal forces of necessity (Cf. C.E. Palmer's philological notes in his edition of *The Oedipus Coloneus of Sophocles*, 1860, 53-55). The discord between the two perspectives is carried up in the dual valence of the German *Glücklich*, which is "happy" in the sense of joyous and, equally, "happy" in the sense of lucky or fortunate. The one denotes a subjective experience, the other a basically external fact. *Glücklich*, then, holds within it the tension between these two tragic visions: in the one, happiness may be a negotiated achievement, but in any event, it is an explicitly personal reality; in the other, happiness is a facet of being, determined more or less in advance of one's personal existence and largely external to who one is. So, Aeschylus, Nietzsche here observes, emphasizes the sublime connection between divine justice and human happiness, while Sophocles declares the sublimity of a necessity almost more than divine in the rigid impersonality with which it distributes happy and unhappy fates.

27. As Karl Jaspers notes in *Nietzsche: Einführung in das Verständnis seines Philosophierens*, by the time of *Thus Spoke Zarathustra*, "Unlike the saint ... Nietzsche would remain in the world and serve the actually human ... it is to him reprehensible that saints 'wished to flee into a beyond, rather than build for a future'" (1981, 124). We see, in his working-out of the theory of the tragic artist, the beginnings of Nietzsche's long effort to come to terms with his own *Ekel* or disgust at humanity, and thereby to discover and serve something that

would be "actually human." Already here, then, Nietzsche parts ways with Schopenhauer, for whom the saint or ascetic—turning back from willing in a flash of disgusted insight, whilst in the very throes of altruistic ecstasy—represents the high point of human existence.

28. It bears mention here, given the importance of the relation between truth, *Wahrheit*, and *Schein*, seeming, that the working of the eye itself is a *Wahr-nehmung*, the taking of something as true or real. I follow standard practice in translating the verb *wahrnehmen* with "perceive," but the reader should keep in mind the bifurcation between *Schein* and *Sein*, seeming and being, implicitly present in the fact that German "perception" *takes* something *as* true. It is against this bifurcation, coded in the very language of perception, that Nietzsche struggles. Also of note here is Nietzsche's extraordinary anticipation of what we have come only lately to call mirror neurons. Cf. Marco Iacobani, "Imitation, Empathy, and Mirror Neurons," in *Annual Review of Psychology 60*: 653-670 (2009).

29. If the Nietzschean perspective anticipates contemporary neuroscience, it is just as prescient as regards the other great manifestation of psychology in the present era. Consider this moment alongside Lacan's eventual dictum: "A signifier is that which represents the subject for another signifier" (1966, 299).

30. Addition by Giorgio Colli and Mazzino Montinari in the *Kritische Studienausgabe*.

31. This list of symptoms of pain follows those typically found in early mid-century German texts on medicine and homeopathic healing. C.f. Ernst Ferdinand Rückert, *Systematische Darstellung aller bis jetzt homöopathischen Arzneien* (1830); Wrelen and D.H., *Der homöopathische Rathgeber bei allen Krankheiten der Menschen* (1836); Theodor Stürmer, *Zur Vermittelung der Extreme in der Heilkunde* (1836). Nietzsche leaves off using commas midway through the list in the original. The particular list in question, though, appears to be drawn from Eduard von Hartmann's *Philosophie des Unbewussten*, which first appeared shortly before "The Dionysian Vision of the World," in 1868. Though the ordering is somewhat different, Hartmann writes that pain can be "continuous or intermittent, burning, freezing, pressing, throbbing, sticking, biting, tearing, wincing, thrilling, and can display an infinity of variations that do not allow of description at all" (1882, 210). As Crawford has shown (1988, *passim*; 1997, 73-74), Hartmann's self-taught, will-heavy philosophy strongly influenced the way Nietzsche came to term's with the intellectual legacy of Schopenhauer. Perhaps most critical here is Hartmann's discussion of the *begleitende Vorstellungen*, "accompanying presentations," that give meaning to pleasure or displeasure as these feelings apprehend a world, but that are not, per Nietzsche, adequate to communicate the "stirring of the will" itself. Nietzsche thus contrasts rhythmics and dynamics, as musical modes of communicating "accompanying presentations," with harmony, which is that through which music imparts "the proper being of the Will" as such.

32. The intellection of the *Begriff* or "concept" has a fundamentally physical dimension—it is that which is grasped, from *greifen*, to grasp or seize or take hold of—but, even more, it implies a subject over and above, outside of that which is grasped. In the world-encompassing sphere of harmony, as expression of the pure essence of the will (in Nietzsche's special sense of "will"), no appearances or phenomena (*Erscheinungen*) are available to an individual will that would stand outside and grasp (*begreifen*) them; the concept (*Begriff*) is rendered powerless within harmony's symbolism of the world, which includes within itself all willing and all grasping.

33. I here render *Schrei* as "scream," not without reference to Edvard Munch's "The Scream" (*Der Schrei der Natur*, "The Scream of Nature"), so often read as a negotiation of Nietzschean themes.

34. Language, *Sprache*, is constructed from the simple past of the verb *sprechen*, to speak; in a strong sense, then, language is "the spoken." The resonance and tone of the spoken are immediately present in language, conceived from this perspective; Nietzsche's position is striking for the way it adds to this the basic "gestural symbolism" of the very movements of the mouth in speaking. Nietzsche's nascent philosophy of language finds illuminating discussion in Claudia Crawford's discussion of her translation of the piece, "'The Dionysian Worldview': Nietzsche's Symbolic Languages and Music" (1997) and in her *The Beginnings of Nietzsche's Theory of Language* (1988).

35. Here once more, the multiple valences of *Ton* and *tönen* should be borne in mind, not least the sense in which these involve the drawing out of something. Cf. n8 *supra*.

36. "Fanatics," "swarmers," or "the fanatic or swarmer," *Schwärmer* is a historically laden term. Martin Luther coined the pejorative *Schwärmerei* to devalue radical cleric Thomas Müntzer and his followers, in particular, and theologies of peasant revolt, in general; Herder pressed the term into service for attacks on Enlightenment philosophy, which he regarded as a coldly collective debility of judgment; and Kant devoted no small effort to distinguishing between the delusional *Schwärmer* with his lunatic visions and the creative rationality of *Enthusiasmus*, the ambiguous presence of fantasy or inflammations of the will within the scope of proper moral sentiments. In negatively valenced usages, *Schwärmer* marks a loss of individual judgment, often in the development of a hive mentality. Fanatics or "swarmers," be they Enlightenment philosophers or revolting peasants, are living in the grip of madness, no longer acquainted with reality. Needless to say, that understanding of *Schwärmer* is one of the applecarts Nietzsche is bent on upsetting. Among many treatments of this key historical-philosophical term, of particular note is Alberto Toscano's *Fanaticism: On the Uses of an Idea* (2010; esp. xiv-xvii, which offers an excellent etymological discussion of "swarmers," "enthusiasts," and "fanatics," and 121-27, on Kant and the *Schwärmer*).

Friedrich Nietzsche was born in 1844 in Röcken, Germany. The stormy period of his intellectual youth included the turbulent friendship with Richard Wagner and love for Cosima Wagner that so influenced this 1870 essay. Between then and before his descent into madness in 1889 and early demise in 1890, Nietzsche was for ten years—from 1869 to 1879—a professor of philosophy at the University of Basel, Switzerland. During this time and thereafter, he wrote a dazzling array of books and innumerable shorter texts, including *The Birth of Tragedy (out of the Spirit of Music)* (1872), *Human, All Too Human* (1878), *Daybreak* (1881), *The Gay Science* (1882/1887), *Thus Spoke Zarathustra* (1883-1885), *Beyond Good and Evil* (1886), *On the Genealogy of Morals* (1887), *The Case of Wagner* (1888), *Twilight of the Idols* (1888), *The Antichrist* (1888), *Ecce Homo* (1888), and *Nietzsche contra Wagner* (1888).

Friedrich Ulfers is Associate Professor in the Department of German at New York University. He has been the recipient of numerous teaching awards, including a Distinguished Teaching Medal, and most recently was granted the German government highest civilian award, the Federal Order of Merit, First Class. He is also founder of the Friedrich Ulfers Prize promoting German-language literature, in conjunction with New York's preeminent German-language literary festival, Festival Neue Literatur. Ulfers has also served as Friedrich Nietzsche Professor and as Dean of the Media and Communication division at the European Graduate School. His essays on Nietzsche, Robert Musil, and other figures of German literary modernity have been published in numerous venues.

Ira Allen is a doctoral candidate in Rhetoric and Composition at Indiana University. He has written articles on political theory and rhetoric and his previous translations have appeared in such publications as *Modern Language Notes* and *The Oxford International Encyclopedia of Legal History*.

Jason Wagner, Drew S. Burk
(Editors)
Univocal Publishing
123 North 3rd Street, #202
Minneapolis, MN 55401
www.univocalpublishing.com

ISBN 9781937561024
This work was composed in Minion and Trajan.
All materials were printed and bound
in October 2013 at Univocal's atelier
in Minneapolis, USA.

The paper is Mohawk Via, Pure White Linen.
The letterpress cover was printed
on Lettra Fluorescent.
Both are archival quality and acid-free